DIGITAL
SISTERHOOD

DIGITAL SISTERHOOD

A Memoir
of
Fierce Living Online

Ananda Kiamsha Madelyn Leeke

iUniverse LLC
Bloomington

Digital Sisterhood
A Memoir of Fierce Living Online

iUniverse books may be ordered through booksellers or by contacting:

iUniverse LLC
1663 Liberty Drive
Bloomington, IN 47403
www.iuniverse.com
1-800-Authors (1-800-288-4677)

ISBN: 978-1-4917-0639-8 (sc)
ISBN: 978-1-4917-0641-1 (hc)
ISBN: 978-1-4917-0640-4 (ebk)

Printed in the United States of America

iUniverse rev. date: 09/20/2013

CONTENTS

EPIGRAPH

"We write our stories with the hope they will be read, and with the hope that readers will have a response. That they will be moved. And whether they respond in ways we expect, or ways we didn't expect, the main thing to remember is that we have written down our experience. And the main movement that occurs is beyond whether or not the books fly off the shelves. The main movement is what occurs within us, the transformation of memory into prose, and in the process becoming conscious of what your life actually is, and who you actually are." Nancy Wait, author of *The Nancy Who Drew* and founder of The Alchemy of Memoir blog

"Digital sisterhood is a state of mind. It is about empowerment and respecting diversity." Jacqui Chew, founder of iFusion Marketing

"Digital sisterhood means that women feel like they have a safe space to say what they want to say." Ebony Utley, Ph.D., Assistant Professor of Communication Studies at California State University, Long Beach, author, *Ms.* blogger, and 2012 Digital Sister of the Year

"Digital sisterhood allows us to connect with each other outside of our comfort zone." Danica Kombol, founder of Beirut or Bust: Curious Travel Adventures and Random Thoughts blog, co-founder and managing partner of Everywhere, and 2012 Digital Sister of the Year

"Digital sisterhood is all I had. When I was blogging, I was writing to my sisters." Stacey Milbern, founder of Crip Chick blog and 2011 Digital Sister of the Year

"Digital sisterhood is the kind of sisterhood that can be created without knowing somebody in person, but knowing them through media. It is the sharing about sisterhood, and the creation and connection of sisterhood in digital media." Reverend Monica A. Coleman, Ph.D., Associate Professor of Constructive Theology and African American Religions at Claremont School of Theology, author, founder of Beautiful Mind blog, and 2012 Digital Sister of the Year

"Digital sisterhood is females who are connected through energy rather than blood. And you know energy passes much greater distances and is much lighter, and much more powerful." Willa Shalit, artist, author, founder of Fairwinds Trading, co-founder of Maiden Nation, and 2012 Digital Sister of the Year

"Digital sisterhood for a lot of folks is the first time that they can find new tribes locally. Digital sisterhood is taking sisterhood and magnifying it because now you can go and find all types of people who have similar interests, and build communities offline." Julie Diaz-Asper, Chief Executive Officer and co-founder of GigGoin and Social Lens Research, and 2012 Digital Sister of the Year

"Digital sisterhood is a movement and it is an extension of the movements that came before it." Karon Jolna, Ph.D., Research Scholar at the University of California at Los Angeles' Center for the Study of Women, and Program Director for *Ms.* in the Classroom

DEDICATION

My womanline

My first digital sister, Theresa B. Leeke

My "digital native" niece, Jordan E. Moss

My "Beijing" digital sisters, Tanya Francois Lewis and Agnes "Rosebud" Roseboro

My Blogalicious digital sisters, Stacey Ferguson and Xina Eiland

My BlogHer digital sisters, Elisa Camahort Page, Jory Des Jardins, and Lisa Stone

My Everywhere digital sisters, Danica Kombol, Tamara Knechtel, and Britton Edwards

My Digital Sisterhood Network sisters

My digital sisters who made their life transition, Erica Kennedy (@ ericajk), Susan Niebur (@whymommy), and Miranda Parker (@ deegospel)

My digital sisters who cultivate connection and build community:
AARP Kitchen Cabinet Bloggers, Art Every Day Month Community,
BAP Living, Black Author Showcase, Black Business Women
Online, Blerdology, Blogalicious, Blogging While Brown, BlogHer,
BlissDom, CRAVE Company, DC Social Media Facebook Group,
Digital Undivided, Fabulous Women Business Owners DC Facebook
Group, Feminism 2.0, Heart of Haiti Bloggers, Hot Mommas
Project, DiversiTech, iVillage, Latinos in Social Media, Little Pink
Book, Next Chapter Book Blogging Club, NiaOnline, Owning Pink,
PinChat—Pinterest Chat Facebook Group, Pink Heels Community
of Women Business Owners, PRENEUR, Quirky Black Girls, She's
Geeky, SheWrites, Sigma Gamma Rho Authors Facebook Group,
Sigma Gamma Rho Professional Women Facebook Group, Social
Media Club DC, Social Media Week DC, Sojournals Urban Media
Network, Tech Women Unite Facebook Group, and Women Grow
Business Facebook Group

Women I have met and connected with online and offline

Women and girls who use technology and those who need more
access and training

ACKNOWLEDGEMENTS

Writing this book has been an act of surrender that reminded me of a lesson my parents taught me: be unapologetically authentic, fierce, and human. It has also been a collaborative process that happened with Creator's love, energy, guidance, power, and resources. I am eternally grateful to Creator for these blessings and the people who have helped me during my writing and publishing journey.

Deep bow of gratitude to my parents, Theresa and John "J" Leeke, family, friends, spiritual communities at All Souls Unitarian Church and the People of Color Sangha of Insight Meditation Community of Washington, D.C., Mastermind Group members, yoga family at Embrace yoga studio and Tranquil Space yoga studio, and creativity coaching and yoga clients. You always give me an abundant supply of love, positive energy, prayers, space, and support! I appreciate and love you all!

I am so thankful for my mother. She is the first person who taught me how to be unapologetically authentic, fierce, and human. She is also the main reason I am plugged into technology. She invested in my tech education by making sure I had my own word processor to keep me company on late nights during my final year of law school way back in 1988. It was a laptop before laptops were around. She also insisted I get an AOL email account in the early 1990s and join Facebook in 2008 (she was on it way before me!).

My father deserves a special shout out for providing consistent and beyond the call of duty support during my writing process. Thank you "J" for being a "ride or die" kind of father, friend, and fan! I could not do it without you!

Many blessings to Team Ananda for supporting me: Michael Bush, my accountant; Boni Candelario, career strategy and empowerment coach; Evette Chambers, my loctician at City Kinks; Dariela Cruz, my graphic designer; Don Diggs, my acupuncturist; Xina Eiland, my PR Coach; Yael Flusberg, my copy editor, life coach, and yoga teacher; Wayne P. Henry, my book editor; Danica Kombol, my branding mentor; Tracy Mickens Hundley, my copy editor; Faith Hunter, my yoga teacher; Leigh Mosley, my photographer; Danielle Polen, my yin yoga teacher; Kimberley Shults, my copy editor; Lauren Medlock Smith, my attorney; and Judy Weathers, my financial advisor. You are my anchors!

Words cannot begin to express the gratitude I have for my book editor and best friend, Wayne P. Henry. We've been on this writing journey since 2002. It has produced three books I could not have done without you, Wayne! Your support, insightful comments and suggestions, and friendship are true blessings!

Sometimes all you need are a few good women who love words and have the patience and skill to read your writing with last minute deadlines. Those women are my extraordinary copy editors Yael Flusberg, Tracy Mickens Hundley, and Kimberley Shults; my career strategy and empowerment coach Boni Candelario; and my branding mentor Danica Kombol. Ladies, I am so grateful for your friendship, presence, and ability to make my words shine. You make me a better writer!

My financial advisor, Judy Weathers, is one of the main reasons I have learned to successfully manage my finances. Judy, your expertise, guidance, and support over the past 11 years have helped me flourish as an author and artist. Thank you from my financial heart!

My body, mind, spirit, and heart are balanced each month through the support of my amazing and grounded acupuncturist, Don Diggs. Don, you have helped me clear my mind, deepen my meditation practice, open my heart to my creativity, and heal and strengthen my body, emotions, and spirit. Thank you and Om Shanti!

Being surrounded by a group of my brothalove friends HKB FiNN, Benjamin (Kenny Dust) Jackson, Shayne Lee, Fred Mays (my NYC Dad), Jason Randolph, Willard A. Stanback, and Ken ("Kensan") Yamaguchi-Clark and receiving their positive feedback and support has been invaluable.

A ton of thanks to Shanti Norris and the Smith Center for Healing and the Arts staff, artists-in-residence, participants, and patrons for always giving me room to expand my creativity as an artist and an amazing space for my many author photo shoots.

Sincere appreciation for my writing mentors Marita Golden, M.J. Ryan, and Gail Straub for giving me the much needed push to write this book the way I was called to . . . authentically.

Blessings of thanksgiving to Grace Ogden and the Sacred Circles community for believing in my creative and healing arts gifts and offering me numerous opportunities to share them.

Very thankful for Julie Diaz Asper, Boni Candelario, Britton Edwards, Xina Eiland, Kety Esquivel, Stacey Ferguson, Judith Hudgins, Danica Kombol, Sharon Malachi, and Alma Suarez for providing feedback on the badges, logos, and web sites for my Ananda Leeke brand and Digital Sisterhood Network community.

My heart is filled with appreciation for the Digital Sisterhood Network community and all of my digital sisters and brothers. Your sharing and support mean the world to me.

Special thanks to my Kickstarter crowdfunding donors for investing in my book project and having patience with my creative process: Mitchell Abdullah, Mari Alonso, Jade Andwele, Veronica Arreola, Monica Barnett, Margaux Delotte Bennett, Tara Betts, Holly Buchanan, Robin Caldwell, Boni Candelario, Nicole Cutts, Corrie Davidson, Sloane Berrent Davidson, Danielle DiPirro, Aimee Dixon, R. Dudley, Britton Edwards, Xina Eiland, Kimberly Ellis, Kety Esquivel, Richael Faitful, Stacey Ferguson, Faydra Fields, Tanya Fields, Adrienne Fikes, Jill Foster, Kiratiana Freelon, Sabrina L. Gray, Cecilia and Andre Harris, LaShanda Henry, Maura Hernandez, Terri Holley, Tameka Kee, Danica Kombol, Diana Kurcfeld, Yalanda Lattimore, John and Theresa Leeke, Marie Legette, Ariane Leigh, Sharon Malachi, Kerrie Martin, Aisha Massac, Richard McCarson, Nancy McCormick, Tracy Chiles McGhee, McGruderCares, Natalie McNeal, Arielle Palmer, Pamela Pressley, Rash, Akilah Richards,

Kamaria Richmond, Evelyn Robinson, Joy Rose, Nadia Ballas Ruta, La Sarmiento, Willa Shalit, Nyasha Smith, Willard Alonzo Stanback, Sonya Steele, Nichelle Stephens, Harold Taylor, Aisha Turman, Lamar and Ronnie Tyler, Johanna Vondeling, Gloria Ware, Kenneth H. Waters, Monda Webb, Joanna White, Jeshawna Wholley, Ora Wiseman, Kim "Soulful" Woods, Veronica Woods, and Takeyah Young.

A bouquet of gratitude to Blogalicious co-founder Stacey Ferguson; BlogHer co-founders, Elisa Camahort Page, Jory Des Jardins, and Lisa Stone; BlogHer staff members Shannon Carroll and Lori Luna; BlissDom co-founders Barbara Jones and Alli Worthington; Latinos in Social Media founder Ana Roca Castro; and Spelman College family Dr. Beverly Daniel Tatum, Dr. Ayoka Chenzira, Tomika DePriest, and Lauren Brown Jarvis for giving me a platform to speak and share my experiences, gifts, and talents with their communities.

Deep appreciation for the women of AARP blogging campaigns, Everywhere, Macy's Heart of Haiti campaign, Maiden Nation, The Mission List, Women Online, and Violet Boutique for collaborating with me on campaigns and events.

Warm and fuzzy gratitude hugs for the wonderful digital communities that have informed, inspired, and influenced my online journey, self-discovery process, and growth as an artist, author, blogger, coach, entrepreneur, innerpreneur, Internet geek, and yoga teacher: Art Every Day Month Community, BAP Living, Black Author Showcase, Black Business Women Online, Blerdology, Blogalicious, Blogging While Brown, BlogHer, BlissDom, CRAVE Company, DC Social Media Facebook Group, Digital Undivided, Fabulous Women Business Owners DC Facebook Group, Feminism 2.0, Heart of Haiti Bloggers, Hot Mommas Project, DiversiTech, iVillage, Latinos in Social Media, Little Pink Book, Next Chapter Book Blogging Club, NiaOnline, Owning Pink, PinChat—Pinterest Chat Facebook Group, Pink Heels Community of Women Business Owners, PRENEUR, Quirky Black Girls, She's Geeky, SheWrites, Sigma Gamma Rho Authors Facebook Group, Sigma Gamma Rho Professional Women Facebook Group, Social Media Club DC, Social

Media Week DC, Sojournals Urban Media Network, Tech Women Unite Facebook Group, and Women Grow Business Facebook Group.

Thank you shout outs to my 16ᵗʰ & U Street Starbucks family for taking good care of me during my writing journey: Matt Beard, Sherie Billingsle, Marcelus Collins, Lauren Cooper, Desmond Davis, Logan Hillman, Rebecca Holdel, Timothy Holland, Diantha Jones, Jonathan Mewborn, Angela Ralph, Betty Russell, Jeremy Simon, Wil Suddrth, Arianna Touissaint, Aja Walton, Julian Wells, and Lakia Young.

My sincere appreciation to the owners and staff at my favorite places to read, write, and dine in my neighborhood: Jolt 'n' Bolt, Regent Thai, Sweet Green, Teaism, The Mediterranean Spot, and Whole Foods.

Many thanks to Barry Lee and the iUniverse team for publishing my third book. It has been a pleasure working with you!

© Leigh Mosley

WELCOME TO MY WORLD WIDE WEB

Welcome to my World Wide Web. It's called *Digital Sisterhood: A Memoir of Fierce Living Online.*

It's August 2013. Twenty-seven years ago this month I started my online journey. My imagination is in full swing, just like it was all those years ago. Today, it travels deeply into a daydream, where I see myself calling you, the reader, on my smartphone to have a conversation about what you will discover in this book.

Here's what I'd tell you: This book is a collection of reflections and stories that celebrate my identity as a proud member of the digital generation. It explores how the Internet and various women have influenced, informed, and inspired my career reinvention, community-building efforts, creative expression, entrepreneurship, learning opportunities, "live your best life" D.C. lifestyle, passion for social media and technology, self-care practices, self-discovery journey, social good activism, thought leadership, and travel adventures.

Digital Sisterhood: A Memoir of Fierce Living Online starts with an introduction to the women who came before me. A cadre of female ancestors who loved to communicate. I call them my womanline. I paint a picture of what I think their digital footprint would have looked like. I also introduce you to my mother, Theresa B. Leeke, through a snapshot look into her online life and how it has influenced mine.

Through my stories and reflections, you'll witness key moments on my Internet Geek path, including the day my digital footprint was born when I logged onto the LexisNexis research service as a first-year law student at Howard University School of Law. You'll travel with me to the United Nations Fourth World Conference on Women in Beijing, China, and discover how a visit to an Internet café changed my life. A series of conversations and interactions I had with a diverse group of women will show you how I embraced my creative expression and career reinvention. Many of these women became my digital diva sheroes and virtual mentors. Their experiences and insights helped me use the Internet as a self-discovery tool and identify seven Digital Sisterhood leadership archetypes I used to shape my roles as a social media leader. They include:

- A Creativista is a woman who gives birth to creativity (art, books, content, films, mobile apps, products, services, webisodes, and videos).

- An Empirista is a woman who thinks of herself as CEO of her own corporation, ME, Inc.; maintains an entrepreneurial mindset; and gives birth to ideas and transforms them into businesses, economies, institutions, networks, and organizations that add value to people's lives.

- An Enchantista is a woman who taps into the magic of her spirit as she focuses her energy, opens her heart, trusts her intuition, embraces her fears, and shares her gifts in service to others.

- An Empowerista is a woman who creates and curates content, shares information and experiences, connects with others and establishes positive relationships, and builds and participates in communities that empower her and others.

- An Evangelista is a woman who supports and advocates a philosophy, a values system, a lifestyle, a cause, or a campaign that improves her life and others' lives.

- A Flowista is a woman who unplugs from her digital life and tech devices for periods of time so she can recharge and take care of her own needs; and encourages women to unplug from their digital lives by incorporating mindfulness and self-care practices.

- A Lifestylista is a woman who lives her life as a work of art; expresses it through her passion for beauty, entertaining, fashion, food, home décor, personal style, and travel; and inspires others to live their lives as works of art.

My blogging and social media adventures will highlight the lessons I have learned while tapping into the power of my archetypes, the reasons I launched the Digital Sisterhood Network, and the experiences that caused me to adopt what I term "fierce living" commitments.

At the end of each chapter, you'll have an opportunity to explore aspects of your own Digital Sisterhood journey through a series of interactive exercises. You'll also have a chance to use the Digital Sisterhood Notes Section for responding to the exercises, journaling "aha!" moments, and jotting down golden nuggets of wisdom. For those of you who are interested in going a bit further, I have included Appendices that invite you to deepen your Digital Sisterhood experience with more exercises and resources.

May my reflections and stories inspire you to explore, celebrate, share, and publish your own Digital Sisterhood journey, embrace fierce living, and become too bold for boundaries!

© *Leigh Mosley*

PART ONE

FIERCE LIVING 1.0

"The Net offers us a chance to take charge of our own lives and to redefine our roles as citizens of local communities and of a global society." Esther Dyson, author of Release 2.1: A Design for Living in the Digital Age

"The Internet is like outerspace; wide open and ready to be conquered." Angel Laws, author of Angel's Laws of Blogging

CHAPTER ONE

IMAGINING THE DIGITAL FOOTPRINT OF MY WOMANLINE

> *"Writing is our footprint in the world."* *Edwidge Danticat,*
> *author of* Create Dangerously: The Immigrant Artist at
> Work

Haitian author Edwidge Danticat's wisdom about a writer using her craft to document her footprint in the world reminds me of the footprints laid by my foremothers. My foremothers who I call my womanline were a tribe of women born with the gift of gab. As consummate communicators, they turned phrases that kept people's minds spinning, told stories sprinkled with wisdom and family history, spoke their truth because it was the only thing they knew how to do, held court on their front porches to keep up with neighborhood and church news, debated issues and advocated for causes near and dear to their hearts, and preached the gospel according to their lives to folks on the other end of the telephone. If they had access to the Internet and social media, what would their digital footprint look like? How many people would have benefited from their wisdom?

My great-grandmother Eunice Ann Thomas Roberts was a church and community leader, an entrepreneur with a thriving business as a tailor, a fashionista, an African American history enthusiast, a wife, and a mother living in Terre Haute, Indiana in the early 1900s. She always had something to say on her front porch that caused people to come and listen. Today, her front porch speeches and conversations would be live streamed as a weekly Ustream.tv talk show called "Mrs. Eunice Ann Roberts' Front Porch." People would use the Twitter hashtag #FrontPorch to live tweet the show. They would post their comments about the show on the Front Porch Facebook Fan page. The videos of the shows would be uploaded to YouTube and Vimeo. Digital Chick TV and Mingle Media TV Network would air the webisodes and promote them as woman-centered web TV.

Eunice Ann's tailoring business would have a WordPress site to offer tips and special deals, and to connect with her customers. She would use Square, the mobile payment solution, on her HTC smartphone to accept credit card payments from her clients. Victoria Colligan's LadiesWhoLaunch.com, Jill Foster's WomenGrowBusiness. com, Cynthia Good's TheLittlePinkBook.com, and LaShanda Henry's Black Business Women Online would be some of her favorite business web sites to visit while sitting at her iMac in her office.

Her passion for classic fashion and accessories would make her a fan of TownandCountryMag.com and HarpersBazaar.com. She would follow the chic fashion moves of First Lady Michelle Obama by reading fashion blogs like Essence.com's First Lady Style, Mary Tomer's Mrs-O.org, and Chanel Ward's MichelleOStyle. Blogspot.com. Commander in Chic author Mikki Taylor's "Mikki-isms" on beauty and style would dominate her Twitterstream. MichelleObamaWatch.com would also be included in her list of favorite Michelle Obama-inspired online destinations.

Her deep interest in African American history would lead her to visit BlackHistory.com. She would use the web site to conduct her research on African American history makers in Indiana. She would also use the Internet to explore her Native American heritage. Places like the Museum of Native American History, AmericanIndian.net, and NativeWeb.org would be bookmarked on her computer.

Just like Eunice Ann, my great-grandmother Florida Jones ("Florida J.") Leeke would be knee deep in the Internet with the support of her two sisters, Lillian and Lavinia. These three women were socialites in Gary and Indianapolis, Indiana, who liked to look good, entertain, and champion causes and organizations that supported African American women and their families. They'd use their Dell laptops to visit Marie Denee's The Curvy Fashionista blog and Kathryn Finney's The Budget Fashionista blog for fashion and style tips. BSmith.com and MarthStewartLiving.com would be their go-to source for entertaining tips. Jennifer James' Mom Bloggers for Social Good site and Tracey Webb's BlacksGivingBack.com would help them with their philanthropic efforts. I know they would email their network of family, friends, and colleagues information about signing online petitions that supported their favorite causes. They would also use online fundraising tools like ChipIn, Crowdrise, GoFundMe, and Indiegogo to raise money for their pet projects and organizations like Sigma Gamma Rho Sorority, Inc., the sorority Florida J. and Lillian joined in the 1930s. Florida J. and Lillian would be active members of their local Sigma Gamma Rho Sorority chapter's Facebook page. LinkedIn would be one of their favorite social networking sites because of its professional nature. They would adore Google+ because they could organize their contacts into Google Circles and host Google Hangout video chats with them. iMeet would be their favorite conference call platform for sorority meetings. Yahoo Groups and Google Docs would help them work as a team with their sorority sisters.

Florida J.'s younger sister, Susan Jones, a poet and a writer (like me) in Indiana and Kentucky, would adore Barnes & Noble's Nook Color tablet and its app, web browsing, and video features because it would allow her to read books and newspapers; stay updated on writing opportunities and resources by visiting BooksbyWomen. org, PoetsandWriters.com and WritersDigest.com; and participate in online writing communities like Black Author Showcase and SheWrites.com. It would also allow her to have a Twitter account and follow a multicultural group of writers like the women listed below.

My aunt, Lillian Jane Leeke Schell ("Aunt Jane"), Florida J.'s daughter, was a world traveler and a French teacher in Gary, Indiana. Social media would enhance Aunt Jane's travel adventures tremendously and cause her to launch a second career as a travel and lifestyle blogger with an iPad, a Tumblr blog, an Instagram account, a Flickr photo sharing account, a Pinterest page, and a YouTube video channel. Her smartphone would help her access the Town & Country Luxury City Guide app to get suggestions for her trips. Foursquare would be her BFF (best friend forever) as she checked into cultural landmarks, restaurants, shops, and hotels to obtain special discounts and offers. Jetsetter.com, TravelandLeisure.com, and American Airlines' BlackAtlas.com would hire her to blog about her travel experiences. She would probably tap into the Leeke family entrepreneurial tradition and use Amazon.com's CreateSpace to self-publish her blogs as travel guide e-books that people could read on their Kindle, Nook, and iPad. Her favorite travel Twitter buddies would be The Passport Party Project founder Tracey Friley @ onebrowngirl and Kiratiana Freelon @kiratiana, author of *Kiratiana's Travel Guide to Black Paris*.

Florida J.'s daughter-in-law Frederica ("Freddie") Stanley Roberts Leeke, my grandmother, loved sharing photos with her sisters, Mabel and Paulyne while they were living in Washington, D.C. Nowadays, Freddie would have an iPhone with an Instagram app that cross—posted her photos on Facebook so family and friends could enjoy moments from her life. I even think she would've created a coffee table book of family photos using Blurb.com, a global creative publishing platform. Her techie family and friends would be excited to view her book with Blurb.com's app for the iPhone and iPad. Since she loved reading newspapers and magazines, sharing current events, and giving her opinion, I know she would post comments on TheRoot.com, WashingtonPost.com, and Oprah.com. Her fingers would joyously click the Facebook "like" button on articles posted on these sites. They would appear on her Facebook wall and the walls of family and friends. As a conversationalist extraordinaire, she would happily embrace the title of lifestyle blogger and use the VoiceBo app to post audio blogs featuring her commentary on everything she encountered in her daily life. She'd win blogging awards and attend social media conferences like BlissDom, Blogalicious, BlogHer, Blog World, Lavish, and SXSW as a panelist who discussed how savvy senior women use social media to enhance life after 70.

Freddie and her sisters, Mabel and Paulyne, adored fashion and accessories like their mother, Eunice Ann. However, Mabel was the most passionate. As a teacher in Elkhart, Indiana, she always made sure she was dressed to the nines and maintained regular hair, manicure, and pedicure appointments. If she were alive today, she would use a Samsung tablet to read Mercedes Sanchez's BeChicMag. com and Yuli Ziv's MyITThings.com. Before she went shopping, she'd mix and match pictures of accessories, clothing, and shoes on Polyvore.com to create a fashion layout displaying her own personal style. Some of her favorite online shopping destinations would include a variety of budget and high-end sites since she liked to get a bargain: Anthropologie.com, AnnTaylorLoft.com, Chicos.com, Kohls.com, Macys.com, Talbots.com, Target.com, and WhiteHouseBlackMarket.com.

Paulyne was a nurse who worked for Freedmen's Hospital (now Howard University Hospital) in Washington, D.C. She promoted healthy eating and nutrition when she cared for me and my three brothers. She would be a big fan of First Lady Michelle Obama's LetsMove.gov. She'd also use the National Women's Health Information Center's WomensHealth.gov. Watching soap operas and movies and sharing family history were some of her favorite things to do. Her HP laptop would maintain bookmarks for *General Hospital* on ABC.com and Netflix's live streaming movies. Ancestry.com would allow her to upload her family history and share it with family members. Keeping in touch with family and friends was extremely important to her. That's why Skype would be her *technology du jour*!

Skype would also play a major role in my grandmother Dorothy ("Nanan") Mae Johnson Gartin's digital life. Nanan loved to talk on the telephone with family and friends who lived near her in Indianapolis, Indiana. She was known for keeping her phone line occupied for numerous hours. Imagine what would happen if she had an iPhone with a Skype app? She would be able to talk to several people at once, see their facial expressions via the video chat, and share neighborhood and family news as she sat in her lounge chair drinking iced tea. She would also eliminate her long-distance phone bill and increase her communication with her daughter, grandchildren, and great grandchildren who live in Illinois, Maryland, Ohio, Pennsylvania, Virginia, and Washington, D.C.

Nanan's mother, Iona Bolden Johnson King, was a farmer's wife who loved to grow and cook her own food in Brown County, Indiana. She was organic and "green" long before it was popular. She would be a staunch supporter of the White House Organic Farm Project and would use her eco-friendly Samsung Replenish smartphone to visit TheWHOFarm.org and stay updated on the program. Her online adventures would include regular visits to Gloria Ware's Black and Into Green blog, Patti Moreno's GardenGirlTV. com, Bianca Alexander's ConsciousLiving.TV, Lynn Miller's OrganicMania.com, and Tracey McQuirter's ByAnyGreensNecessary. com. I'm sure she would join the Green Moms' Blog Carnivals when she felt compelled to speak her mind about green living.

Nanan's mother-in-law, Ida Farmer Gartin, was very active in her local Seventh-Day Adventist Church in Indianapolis, Indiana. She enjoyed traveling with her church throughout the United States. That's why I know she would have used a smartphone and a digital camera to document her travels and activities. She'd probably share them with her family and church members on Facebook, Flickr, Instagram, and Pinterest. The Seventh-Day Adventist Church's SDAnet.org would help her stay informed and connected to her fellow church members.

Theresa, my mother and Nanan's daughter, has been actively creating her digital footprint since the late 1980s in Prince George's County, Maryland. Mommy introduced me to the power of the Internet when she installed Dialog, an online information retrieval system, in her home office so she could do her research for her graduate studies at Trinity College in 1988. She is the reason I started using AOL email in 1995, launched my first web site as an artist and author in 2000, and landed on Facebook in 2008, a few years after she joined. When I was dragging my feet on purchasing a smartphone in 2009, she convinced me to take the leap so I could text, tweet, and respond to email. My mother is the texting queen! She also showed me through her work as a choir director, a liturgical music director, and the president of the D.C. chapter of Sigma Gamma Rho Sorority, how to manage my meetings, my involvement in organizations, and my facilitation of focus groups with Yahoo! Groups, Facebook, and FreeConferenceCall.com. Her consistent online financial support of President Barack Obama's presidential campaign convinced me to donate money too. Her concern for privacy and online identity theft made me more cautious about how I share information. The more she evolves in the digital space, the more I evolve. It's true what they say: "like digital mother, like digital daughter."

Writing Exercise:
Imagining Your Womanline's Digital Footprint

After my digital sister, Xina Eiland, a public relations professional, read the rough draft of this chapter, she sent me an email that discussed her womanline's digital footprint. See below.

> *Date: Sat, July 16, 2011 2:43:15 PM*

> *Girl, I read your emails several times. I started imaging what my grandmother(s) digital footprints would be. Grandmother Eiland's Twitter handle would be @Nimrod because of her deep love for my grandfather. Her Twitter handle had to be his name. Yes, my grandfather was named after Nimrod, a warrior in the Bible who disobeyed God. Don't ask; they are from the South.*

> *Grandmother Ricks' trending topic would be #praiseHISname because of her love for Christ. She would use Twitter as a way to spread the Word and to thank God for everything.*

> *You should start a Twitter discussion on the subject of what our grandmothers, great aunts, godmothers' Twitter handles and trending topics would be if they were alive.*

Get a pen and a piece of paper, or turn on your smartphone, iPad, tablet, netbook, laptop, or desktop computer, and use the question below to explore your female ancestors' digital footprint.

1. What would your womanline's digital footprint look like?
    *   Great Grandmothers
    *   Grandmothers
    *   Mothers
    *   Aunts

- Mother Figures
- Other

2. Here are a few more ideas—consider them extracurricular activities:

    - If you blog, write a post about your womanline's digital footprint and ask your blog audience to comment about their womanline's digital footprint.

    - If you create video, audio blogs, or podcasts, record one about your womanline's digital footprint. Invite your audience to share their video, audio blog, or podcast responses.

    - For Facebook, Google+, and LinkedIn users, strike up a conversation with your family, friends, and colleagues by posting a status update about your womanline's digital footprint. Invite them to share their thoughts.

    - For Google Hangout, Skype, UStream.tv, Spreecast, and live stream users, host a live chat about your womanline's digital footprint. Invite your audience to share their thoughts.

    - For Flickr, Instagram, and Pinterest users, post a photo or image that illustrates your womanline's digital footprint. Encourage your followers to comment and share a photo that represents their womanline's digital footprint.

    - Meet a digital sister face-to-face to chat about the discoveries you made while reading this chapter. Use Facebook or Foursquare to check in at your meet up location. Please be careful when you check in. Perhaps you can do the check in when you are leaving the location for safety precautions. Also, be mindful of how much information you share while checking in. Memorialize your meet up with a photo.

Consider posting it on Facebook, Flickr, Google+, Instagram, LinkedIn, Pinterest, or Twitter after you have left the meet up location.

- Go a step further and tweet about your womanline's digital footprint. Invite your Twitter friends to join the conversation. Use the hashtag #womdigfootprint. Be sure to send me a tweet about your conversation. I am @anandaleeke and @digitalsisterhd on Twitter. See you online!

Digital Sisterhood Notes Section

Feel free to use the following pages to write your responses to the chapter exercises, to journal your aha moments, to record golden nuggets of wisdom, or to take notes on whatever pops up in your gorgeous mind! Happy writing!

Digital Sisterhood Notes Section

Digital Sisterhood Notes Section

Ananda Kiamsha Madelyn Leeke

Digital Sisterhood Notes Section

CHAPTER TWO

TRUTH: I AM MY MOTHER'S DAUGHTER

"Information, media, and technology opened up a new world for me." Theresa B. Leeke

One morning while I was sitting at the 16ᵗʰ and U Starbucks drinking my *Venti* decaf Café Americano with three pumps of raspberry and a dash of my own rice milk, thoughts about my mother Theresa occupied my brain when I should have been writing this book. Little did I know those thoughts would inspire this chapter. Don't you just love how the universe and the creative muse conspire to work it all out?

Musician. Feminist. Sorority Leader. Educator. Traveler. A former paper girl with a newspaper route and dreams of being a radio DJ in Indianapolis, Indiana. These are just a few words that describe my mother. Her passion for information, media, and technology decorated the landscape of my childhood. It started with her listening to an early morning radio show, WTOP-AM. The show provided updates on local news, politics, traffic, weather, and school closings. My mother was in the know 24/7/365.

Her passion embraced the headlines of the *Washington Post* newspaper and the evening news on television. It also greeted me each week when *JET* magazine, the *Indianapolis Recorder* newspaper, and the *Catholic Standard* newspaper arrived in the mailbox. Each month it showed up when her favorite magazines, *Ebony*, *Essence*, and *Ms.* appeared on my family's kitchen table. Because of her voracious media appetite, my brain inhaled it all!

When I turned 13, I developed a healthy appetite for lipstick, fashion, entertainment, and women's issues as a result of reading my mother's *Essence* and *Ms.* magazines, and discovering my own favorites, *Mademoiselle, Glamour, Right On!,* and *Vogue.* All of the articles I read inspired my desire to expand my wardrobe while I was a seventh grader at Kenmoor Junior High School in Landover, Maryland. I begged my parents for money to purchase outfits, shoes, and accessories. My mother told me I would have to make do with what she and my father already purchased unless I found a job. She suggested I consider becoming a paper girl like she was when she was in elementary school because it would allow me to earn my own money and spend it the way I liked. The power of being able to earn and spend my own money excited me. So I talked to my brothers, Mike and Mark, who were ready to retire from delivering the *Washington Star,* the local evening paper. They gave me an opportunity to shadow them on their afternoon route and weekly collection process. It didn't take me long to fall in love with being the neighborhood paper girl. I even expanded my paper delivery enterprise to include the *Washington Post,* the daily morning paper, when I entered the eighth grade. That move helped me acquire a deep desire to always read the Style, Business, and Metro sections before reading any other part of the paper (I still do it today!).

Nowadays, my mother's passion for information, media, and technology is still going strong. Her favorite news sources have expanded to include CNN and MSNBC; the *Washington Post, Washington Afro-American, Washington Informer, Prince George's Journal, Catholic Standard,* and *Indianapolis Recorder* newspapers; and WHUR-FM and WTOP-AM radio stations. Her magazine collection includes *Black Enterprise, Ebony, Essence, Good Housekeeping, Heart and Soul, JET, Prevention, Real Simple, Soap Opera Digest,* and *The Oprah Magazine.*

She has one laptop for her music and work as the director of liturgical music and gospel choir director for her Catholic church. Her second laptop is used to access the Internet, email, online banking, Amazon.com, and her work with Sigma Gamma Rho Sorority, Inc. and the Phyllis Wheatley YWCA. Whenever she travels, one of her laptops goes with her. Her iPod is loaded with gospel music to keep her company. Hotel WiFi service and business centers are essential to making her stay a favorable one.

YouTube is one of her favorite places to visit online. She enjoys watching videos featuring gospel music singers and musicians. They help her prepare and select music for her church's weekly Masses and concerts. She also shares them with her choir members as a way of introducing them to new music.

Facebook is her online community du jour. She uses it to stay in touch with family, friends, former students she taught in the D.C. and Maryland Catholic schools, sorority members, and colleagues. Her Facebook status updates give voice to her spiritual inspirations from Joyce Meyer to Joel Osteen, her feminist perspective and commitment to women's rights, her support of President Barack Obama and First Lady Michelle Obama, her commentary on popular culture, and her sense of humor. Her digital camera allows her to capture, post, and share photos with family and friends on Facebook. Her membership in various Facebook groups fuels her community building spirit.

One of her best friends is her Samsung Galaxy smartphone. It keeps her plugged into her email and accessible via text to family, friends, and people she is working with through her church, sorority, and community organizations. Skype has allowed her to maintain a long distance connection to family and friends who live in other states and countries.

So what's next for my digital diva shero mother? She's busy learning how to use her mini iPad and pursuing her intellectual curiosity for anything that quenches her thirst and passion for information, media, and technology. As for me, I will continue to be my mother's daughter by quenching my thirst and passion for information, media, and technology with my smartphone and apps that help me read email, text messages, tweets, Facebook posts, "Scandal" recaps, "Young and the Restless" summaries, TheRoot.com, and the *Washington Post*. Confession: I still enjoy reading the print version of the *Washington Post Express* while I eat my breakfast and listen to WPFW-FM radio station in my sunny yellow kitchen a few times a week. I love technology, but my monthly magazine reading is old school—except for reading ClutchMagazine.com. Most months, I set aside special time to go to Jolt-n-Bolt Cafe, Sweet Green, Starbucks, Teaism or The Mediterranean Spot to grab a bite to eat and drink tea while my eyes marinate themselves in juicy articles I find in *bitch, ELLE, Experience Life, Fast Company, Glamour, Heart & Soul, Latina, More, Poets & Writers, Prevention, Self, Shape, Shambhala Sun, Whole Living, Wired, Women's Health,* and *Yoga Journal.* I call it my "me" time!

Writing Exercise: Your Digital Diva Sheroes

My mother, Theresa, was the first woman who influenced my passion for information, media, and technology. Many other women have influenced me too. Some I know personally. Most I know from blogs, books, conferences, listservs, magazines, meet ups, newspapers, podcasts, radio shows, social networking sites, webinars, workshops, and videos. I call them my digital diva sheroes.

Get a pen and a piece of paper, or turn on your smartphone, iPad, tablet, netbook, laptop, or desktop computer, and use the questions below to explore your passion for information, media, and/ or technology, and your digital diva sheroes.

1. Do you have a passion for information, media, and/or technology? If so, describe it.
2. Name the women who influenced your passion for information, media, and/or technology.
3. Who are your digital diva sheroes? See Appendices for my list.
4. Here are a few more ideas—consider them extracurricular activities:

   • If you blog, write a post about your digital diva sheros and ask your blog audience to comment about their digital diva sheroes.

   • If you create video, audio blogs, or podcasts, record one that pays tribute to your digital diva sheroes. Invite your audience to share their video, audio blog, or podcast responses.

   • For Facebook, Google+, and LinkedIn users, strike up a conversation with your family, friends, and colleagues by posting a status update about your digital diva sheroes. Invite them to share their thoughts.

- For Google Hangout, Skype, UStream.tv, Spreecast, and live stream users, host a live chat about your digital diva sheroes. Invite your audience to share their thoughts.

- For Flickr, Instagram, and Pinterest users, post photos or images of your digital diva sheroes. Encourage your followers to comment and share photos of their digital diva sheroes.

- Meet a digital sister face-to-face to chat about the discoveries you made while reading this chapter. Use Facebook or Foursquare to check in at your meet up location. Please be careful when you check in. Perhaps you can do the check in when you are leaving the location for safety precautions. Also, be mindful of how much information you share while checking in. Memorialize your meet up with a photo. Consider posting it on Facebook, Flickr, Google+, Instagram, LinkedIn, Pinterest, or Twitter after you have left the meet up location.

- Go a step further and tweet about your digital diva sheroes. Share why they are your sheroes. Invite your Twitter friends to join the conversation. Use the hashtag #digdivasheroes. Be sure to send me a tweet about your conversation. I am @ anandaleeke and @digitalsisterhd on Twitter. See you online!

Digital Sisterhood Notes Section

Feel free to use the following pages to write your responses to the chapter exercises, to journal your aha moments, to record golden nuggets of wisdom, or to take notes on whatever pops up in your gorgeous mind! Happy writing!

Digital Sisterhood Notes Section

Digital Sisterhood Notes Section

Ananda Kiamsha Madelyn Leeke

Digital Sisterhood Notes Section

CHAPTER THREE

IN THE BEGINNING WAS THE CLICK

"I never expected to be a techie" Esther Dyson, author of
Release 2.1: A Design for Living in the Digital Age

Never, and I say never, did I expect to be a techie, geek, or computer
lover. I didn't see it coming. It happened with my first click in 1986.
Terrified is the best word to describe my mental state as I sat watching
my first-year law classmate Lisa turn on a desktop computer in the
Howard University Law Library. I had spent four years at Morgan
State University avoiding computers and the computer lab despite the
warnings of my computer science major roommate that they were an
inevitable part of everyone's future. Her geek girl warning made no
sense to me. What did a French major like me need with a computer?
It was hard to understand (said my inner technophobe). If I touched
it the wrong way, I could easily break it (like the other electronic
gadgets I killed in my past) and pay a fortune to have it fixed. I
thought, *"Hey, it's the 80s and an electric typewriter got me through
high school and college, and will do the same for law school."* My first
legal writing class homework assignment required me to learn how to
use LexisNexis, an online legal research and news database service. It
destroyed my typewriter strategy.

Panic set in as I pulled my chair next to Lisa's. I was about to
lose my digital virginity. She made room for me to sit directly
in front of the computer and guided me as I typed in my log on
information. When I saw the LexisNexis logo appear on the screen,
I imagined a world of danger would follow. We did several practice

searches that were surprisingly easy. Then she showed me how I could access current news from the *Washington Post*. As a self-proclaimed news junkie, that became my *piece de resistance*! My fear of danger disappeared. It was replaced with what I now call the Internet geek thirst. I sat at the computer for the next 45 minutes with a goofy smile plastered across my face and my eyes pressed to the screen scanning a plethora of articles. It was official. I had made my debut as a web-utante (a phrase I discovered while reading the November 2011 issue of *Glamour*)!

The computer and LexisNexis became my new BFFs. My only wish was that we had more time together. I dreamed of having a LexisNexis connection at home. Our relationship deepened during my first summer legal internship at the Lawyers' Committee for Civil Rights Under Law in Boston, Massachusetts. A second-year legal intern taught me how to use LexisNexis to conduct searches about potential employers, a skill I practiced frequently during my fall interviews as a second-year student.

At the end of my second year, I landed a summer law clerk position in the legal department of The MAXIMA Corporation, a computer firm, in Rockville, Maryland. My supervisor, David R. Smith, MAXIMA's General Counsel, assigned me to work with a computer programmer in one of MAXIMA's subsidiaries. My job was to interview the computer programmer and prepare a timeline of facts to support one of MAXIMA's lawsuits. During the process, I developed a basic understanding of computer programming terms and how the subsidiary operated. By the end of the summer, I had become friends with several people who worked for the subsidiary and made a point to stay updated on their work. I used the LexisNexis computer in MAXIMA's legal department to research articles about the topics we discussed.

My third year of law school began with an invitation to extend my MAXIMA law clerkship. There was no hesitation in my voice when I accepted. How could I walk away from an employment experience that felt more like play than work? How could I pass up a chance to learn more about computers? How could I deprive myself of unlimited access to LexisNexis without having to compete with my classmates for time at Howard's Law Library? I couldn't. There was no turning back. My summer MAXIMA crush had developed into a full-blown love affair!

Life got juicier in the middle of my third year when my mother purchased and installed a dial-up research service in her home to make her research as a graduate student in her final year of study easier. When she told me LexisNexis was included in the service, I started catching the subway to her house on the weekends. It got so bad that she had to put me on a schedule so I would not conflict with her online research. That's when I knew I had a full-blown addiction.

Writing Exercise: Your First Time

Get a pen and a piece of paper, or turn on your smartphone, iPad, tablet, netbook, laptop, or desktop computer, and take a walk down digital memory lane by answering the questions below.

1. When was the first time you logged onto the Internet?
2. Where did you travel in cyberspace during your online visit?
3. How did you feel when you explored the Internet for the first time?
4. After you had your first online experience, what did you begin to use the Internet for?
5. How has the Internet impacted your life?
6. Here are a few more ideas—consider them extracurricular activities:

   - If you blog, write a post about your first online experience and ask your blog audience to comment about their experiences.

   - If you create video, audio blogs, or podcasts, record one about your first online experience. Invite your audience to share their video, audio blog, or podcast responses.

   - For Facebook, Google+, and LinkedIn users, strike up a conversation with your family, friends, and colleagues by posting a status update about your first online experience. Invite them to share their thoughts.

   - For Google Hangout, Skype, UStream.tv, Spreecast, and live stream users, host a live chat about your first online experience. Invite your audience to share their thoughts.

   - For Flickr, Instagram, and Pinterest users, post a photo or image that illustrates your first online experience. Encourage your followers to comment and share a photo that represents their first online experience.

- Meet a digital sister face-to-face to chat about the discoveries you made while reading this chapter. Use Facebook or Foursquare to check in at your meet up location. Please be careful when you check in. Perhaps you can do the check in when you are leaving the location for safety precautions. Also, be mindful of how much information you share while checking in. Memorialize your meet up with a photo. Consider posting it on Facebook, Flickr, Google+, Instagram, LinkedIn, Pinterest, or Twitter after you have left the meet up location.

- Go a step further and tweet about your first online experience. Invite your Twitter friends to join the conversation. Use the hashtag #1stonlineexper. Be sure to send me a tweet about your conversation. I am @anandaleeke and @digitalsisterhd on Twitter. See you online!

Digital Sisterhood Notes Section

Feel free to use the following pages to write your responses to the chapter exercises, to journal your aha moments, to record golden nuggets of wisdom, or to take notes on whatever pops up in your gorgeous mind! Happy writing!

Digital Sisterhood Notes Section

Digital Sisterhood Notes Section

Digital Sisterhood Notes Section

PART TWO

FIERCE LIVING 2.0

"Going online isn't really about computers; it's about communication as well as making connections to both information and people."

"Women are online in force, hooking up personally, finding new opportunities professionally, and networking with women all over the world."

Aliza Sherman, author of Cybergrrl!: A Woman's Guide to the World Wide Web

CHAPTER FOUR

A GAME CHANGER:
BEIJING WOMEN'S CONFERENCE

> *"For the first time, there were Internet cafes set up that allowed the attendees to use technology to caucus in real time with their membership back in their native countries."*
> Silicon Valley executive Robin Abrams (served as Apple's managing director in Beijing, China when the company was asked to sponsor the United Nations Fourth World Conference on Women)

By the time I arrived in Beijing, China, to attend the United Nations (UN) Fourth World Conference on Women in 1995, I was 30, owned a condo and a desktop computer, worked as the debt manager in the D.C. Office of the Treasurer, wrote and self-published three chapbooks of poetry, and transformed coat hangers into wire sculptures of women's silhouettes as a mixed media artist by night. My life was calling me to make some changes, but I didn't know how. I was hesitant to answer the call because I couldn't see any light at the end of the tunnel. So I sat on the fence until I decided to travel to China.

After I made my travel arrangements, I met with my supervisor to discuss my leave request. She informed me that she would not be able to approve it because our office was in the midst of handling a new municipal bond transaction. I knew in my heart that I was going to China despite her decision. I shared my decision with her. She explained if I chose my trip I could be terminated.

My choice created unwanted and unnecessary drama in the workplace and anxiety in my emotions as I boarded the plane at John F. Kennedy Airport in New York City with a delegation of African American women, led by my mentor, Barbara R. Arnwine, Executive Director of the Lawyers' Committee for Civil Rights Under Law, and the late Dr. Dorothy I. Height, Chairwoman and former President of the National Council of Negro Women (NCNW). Flashbacks of a conversation I had with Barbara where she convinced me to attend the UN conference after she purchased my first wire sculpture collection for the Black Women and the Law Conference haunted me. I wondered why I listened to her as I settled into my seat. When the plane finally took off, the question no longer mattered. All I could do was surrender to the adventures awaiting me.

During the flight, I met my soon-to-be roommate Sharon, a graduate student studying Public Policy and Women's Studies at George Washington University. We swapped stories about living in the same D.C. neighborhood, the impact of feminism on our lives, and our college and graduate school experiences. By the time we landed in Shanghai, our first stop in China, we were friends. I knew Sharon and I would experience great adventures.

Our first day in Shanghai was spent touring a local hospital that offered traditional Chinese and western medical services, seeing a man receive acupuncture treatment, and meeting Tanya Francois, a Louisiana-born science professional from Boston, and Agnes "Rosebud" Roseboro, a North Carolina-born NCNW officer and social worker from Greensboro. Tanya, "Rosebud," and I bonded on the bus ride to and from the township. They told me stories about their reasons for wanting to attend the UN conference. As I listened, I wondered if I should disclose the details surrounding my participation and the possibility of my job loss. I decided to only share the story about my mentor Barbara insisting I travel to China to expand my understanding of women's rights and different cultures. It was short, sweet, and safe.

A few days later, we traveled to Beijing. When we arrived at the Beijing Grace Hotel, my comfort level with Sharon, Tanya, and "Rosebud" deepened. Each day while we traveled by bus to and from Huairou, the city where the Nongovernmental (NGO) Forum was held, I shared a few more details about my life. Eventually, I told each one of them about the possibility of my job loss. To my surprise, they were very supportive. They helped me begin to accept the advantages and disadvantages of my choice. They never made me feel guilty or stupid. Instead, they reminded me how much courage it took to follow my heart and live my life passionately.

One of the benefits of following my heart and living my life passionately in Beijing was meeting women from all over the world. During the NGO Forum's opening ceremony, I sat with a group of women from Brazil, India, Kenya, Korea, the Netherlands, Russia, Senegal, and Zimbabwe. As the ceremony ended, we stood together and sang Pat Humphies song, "Keep on Moving Forward." Five lines from that song became my mantra and helped me fully embrace my conference experience as a series of life-changing adventures.

> *"Gonna keep on walking forward*
> *Keep on walking forward*
> *Keep on walking forward*
> *Never turning back*
> *Never turning back"*

One of those life-changing adventures happened when I heard former First Lady Hillary Rodham Clinton give her famous "Women's Rights Are Human Rights" speech which included the following remarks:

> *"Those of us who have the opportunity to be here have the responsibility to speak for those who could not.*
>
> *We need to understand that there is no formula for how women should lead their lives. That's why we must respect the choices that each woman makes for herself and her family. If*

> *there is one message that echoes forth from this conference, it*
> *is that human rights—and women's rights are human rights.*
> *Let us not forget that among those rights are the right to*
> *speak freely—and the right to be heard."*

Clinton's words echoed what was in my heart, gave me a clearer understanding of why I was in Beijing, and helped shape my digital path. They came to life when I visited a conference art exhibit organized by the Women's Caucus for Art (WCA), a national member organization of multidisciplinary and multicultural artists, art historians, students, educators, and museum professionals. While I was there, I struck up a conversation with several WCA artists who were overseeing the exhibit. We talked about WCA's role as a NGO and founding member of the Feminist Art Project, the conference, their careers, and my life as a budding artist. Before we parted, they gave me their business cards and encouraged me to visit the WCA web site and join the D.C. Chapter.

Walking with Sharon into the NGO Forum's Internet Café was another life changing adventure. It marked the first time I saw a diverse group of women sitting at computers. My face lit up with a smile as I realized how powerful women could be with Internet access. They were free to speak their minds, discuss their concerns, share information, build community, create web sites and coalitions to address their concerns, and launch advocacy campaigns that defied geographical boundaries. They were demonstrating what Clinton said in her speech: *"Let us not forget that among those rights are the right to speak freely—and the right to be heard."*

As Sharon surfed the web to find information about several women's organizations and emailed her parents and friends, I realized I needed to get an email account and Internet access when I returned home so I could keep in touch with her, Tanya, and "Rosebud," and visit the WCA web site.

Writing Exercises: You've Got Mail

Get a pen and a piece of paper, or turn on your smartphone, iPad, tablet, netbook, laptop, or desktop computer, and retrace your first email conversations with women in your life by answering the questions below.

1. When did you start using email?
2. What was your first email address?
3. Who were the first women you emailed?
4. How did you meet these women (online or IRL—in real life)?
5. What did you discuss during your email conversations?
6. Did your email conversations with other women provide business, career, community, creative, emotional, mentoring, or spiritual support that strengthened your friendships? How so?
7. Have you used email to raise awareness about a causes and campaigns or build coalitions with other women? How so?
8. Here are a few more ideas—consider them extracurricular activities:

   • If you blog, write a post about your first email experiences and ask your blog audience to comment about their experiences.

   • If you create video, audio blogs, or podcasts, record one about your first email experiences. Invite your audience to share their video, audio blog, or podcast responses.

   • For Facebook, Google+, and LinkedIn users, strike up a conversation with your family, friends, and colleagues by posting a status update about your first email experiences. Invite them to share their thoughts.

- For Google Hangout, Skype, UStream.tv, Spreecast, and live stream users, host a live chat about your first email experiences. Invite your audience to share their thoughts.

- For Flickr, Instagram, and Pinterest users, post a photo or image that illustrates your first email experiences. Encourage your followers to comment and share a photo that represents their first email experiences.

- Meet a digital sister face-to-face to chat about the discoveries you made while reading this chapter. Use Facebook or Foursquare to check in at your meet up location. Please be careful when you check in. Perhaps you can do the check in when you are leaving the location for safety precautions. Also, be mindful of how much information you share while checking in. Memorialize your meet up with a photo. Consider posting it on Facebook, Flickr, Google+, Instagram, LinkedIn, Pinterest, or Twitter after you have left the meet up location.

- Go a step further and tweet about your first email experiences. Invite your Twitter friends to join the conversation. Use the hashtag #1emailexper. Be sure to send me a tweet about your conversation. I am @anandaleeke and @digitalsisterhd on Twitter. See you online!

Digital Sisterhood Notes Section

Feel free to use the following pages to write your responses to the chapter exercises, to journal your aha moments, to record golden nuggets of wisdom, or to take notes on whatever pops up in your gorgeous mind! Happy writing!

Ananda Kiamsha Madelyn Leeke

Digital Sisterhood Notes Section

Digital Sisterhood Notes Section

Digital Sisterhood Notes Section

I AM
A
CREATIVISTA
DIGITAL SISTER!
#dscreativista

© *Leigh Mosley*

CHAPTER FIVE

THE BIRTH OF MY INNER CREATIVISTA

"Your creative self is alive and waiting for your invitation to evolve!" Gail McMeekin, *author of* The 12 Secrets of Highly Creative Women

Life after my Beijing adventures moved at a rapid pace. The first day I returned to my job as debt manager, my supervisor notified me she had decided to terminate my employment for failure to obtain leave approval for my trip. She also informed me I had six weeks until my termination took effect and the right to appeal her decision. Her words did not surprise me. They echoed the same message she delivered during a meeting we had before I boarded the plane to China two weeks earlier. The surprise came when I realized I only had six weeks to make the transition to the next chapter of my life.

During my six-week countdown, email became a lifesaver. Hearing the AOL message "You've Got Mail" was a reassuring sound of support coming from my UN Women's Conference friends, "Rosebud" and Tanya. Their email messages were filled with wise counsel, prayers, positive energy, encouragement, and personal stories of how they managed to move through change in their own lives. Although we were physically separated from each other, I felt connected to them. We had become an email network, a community, and an online force that left me feeling understood and affirmed. Looking back, I realize they were my first "Digital Sisterhood" circle of support.

Having their support gave me the courage to dig deeper into the artist and writer I was becoming. Journaling and writing poetry about my experiences at the UN Women's Conference helped me express my emotions. Often, I would send my "Digital Sisterhood" circle of support email messages with short updates about my discoveries. Sometimes, I would include excerpts from my journal entries and poems, and ask for feedback. These ladies always responded generously with insightful comments and questions. A few times, they called me to discuss my work. During each call, they always told me how powerful and valuable my creativity was. They believed in me more than I believed in myself.

In the midst of wrapping up my responsibilities as debt manager and signing up for employment with temporary agencies, I began living the next chapter of my life by carving out time to create artwork, write poetry, and surf the web. The Women's Caucus for Art was one of the first web sites I visited. Each time I visited the site, I was exposed to a new world of possibilities. It made me long for a community of like-minded women artists who were passionate and committed to expressing their creativity.

During one of my site visits, I found the email address for the D.C. chapter and later wrote a carefully crafted message that introduced myself and explained my reasons for wanting to become a chapter member. A few days later, the D.C. chapter membership chair responded with a warm greeting and a copy of the membership application. I printed it out, completed it, and mailed it along with a check for the membership fee. After I became a member, I attended monthly meetings, gained a community of local artists, learned about the business of being an artist, obtained mentors, and participated in art exhibitions. As a result, I was able to embrace my identity as a Creativista, a woman who gives birth to creativity.

Writing Exercises: Your Inner Creativista

Get a pen and a piece of paper, or turn on your smartphone, iPad, tablet, netbook, laptop, or desktop computer, and reflect on how you give birth to creativity by answering the questions below.

1. Whenever I watch Demi Lovato's "Work of Art" music video on YouTube, I am reminded of how important it is for everyone to follow their heart, knowing that their imagination is a gift that can help them dream and give birth to their creativity. How do you express creativity in your life?
2. What YouTube videos and/or songs inspire and/or remind you to honor your creative spirit?
3. Do you have any creative mentors who inspire you in your digital life? Who are they? How do inspire and/or mentor you?
4. How does technology (the Internet, social media, and tech devices and tools) support your creative birthing process?
5. Are you a Creativista? How so?
6. Here are a few more ideas—consider them extracurricular activities:

   • If you blog, write a post about one or more of your responses above and ask your blog audience to share their comments.

   • If you create video, audio blogs, or podcasts, record one about one or more of your responses above. Invite your audience to share their comments on a video, audio blog, or podcast.

   • For Facebook, Google+, and LinkedIn users, strike up a conversation with your family, friends, and colleagues by posting a status update about one or more of your responses above. Invite them to share their thoughts.

- For Google Hangout, Skype, UStream.tv, Spreecast, and live stream users, host a live chat about one or more of your responses above. Invite your audience to share their thoughts.

- For Flickr, Instagram, and Pinterest users, post a photo or image that illustrates one or more of your responses above. Encourage your followers to comment.

- Meet a digital sister face-to-face to chat about the discoveries you made while reading this chapter. Use Facebook or Foursquare to check in at your meet up location. Please be careful when you check in. Perhaps you can do the check in when you are leaving the location for safety precautions. Also, be mindful of how much information you share while checking in. Memorialize your meet up with a photo. Consider posting it on Facebook, Flickr, Google+, Instagram, LinkedIn, Pinterest, or Twitter after you have left the meet up location.

- Go a step further and tweet about one or more of your responses above. Invite your Twitter friends to join the conversation. Use the hashtag #creativista. Be sure to send me a tweet about your conversation. I am @anandaleeke and @digitalsisterhd on Twitter. See you online!

Digital Sisterhood Notes Section

Feel free to use the following pages to write your responses to the chapter exercises, to journal your aha moments, to record golden nuggets of wisdom, or to take notes on whatever pops up in your gorgeous mind! Happy writing!

Digital Sisterhood Notes Section

Digital Sisterhood Notes Section

Digital Sisterhood Notes Section

I AM
AN
EMPIRISTA
DIGITAL SISTER!
#dsempirista

© Leigh Mosley

CHAPTER SIX

Dupont Circle Internet Geek Becomes Empirista

> *"Take what you want out of life, and remember: Each night is as important as every other night; each day is yours for the taking."* Harriet Rubin, *author of* The Princessa: Machiavelli for Women

Today is August 30, 2012. I just filed my business, Kiamsha.com, LLC's two-year report for domestic filing with the Corporations Division of D.C. Government online. As I pressed the button to pay the $400 fee, I remembered four key milestones in my life that set me on the path to being an entrepreneur. The first was in 1976, when I was 12 and began making handmade cards with original poetry for family members and friends. On the back of each card, I included a copyright statement with my business name PL Corp. PL Corp referred to my childhood nickname "Puff," my last name Leeke, and an abbreviation of the word corporation. I got the idea from reading *Black Enterprise*, one of my father's favorite magazines. The second milestone happened when I established my first sole proprietorship, Sunsum Communications, as a publishing house for my poetry chapbooks in 1992. 1993 marked the third milestone when I completed my entrepreneurial training course sponsored by the American Woman's Economic Development Corporation. A series of conversations I had with Catherine Austin Fitts, President of The Hamilton Securities Group, Inc., an employee-owned investment banking and financial software firm that served as lead financial advisor to Federal Housing Administration (FHA), in 1996 was the fourth milestone.

Conversations have the power to change our lives. They can alter who we are and the way we look at ourselves in fundamental ways. When we feel heard and affirmed, they can inspire courage to live authentically and pursue our dreams. They can also be the starting point for mentorship and sponsorship, the dynamic duos in building a business or career. Sometimes we don't notice the impact of these conversations as they are happening. Often, we realize the magnitude of their impact days, weeks, months, or years later. When we have the "aha" moments and connect the dots, we're able to appreciate how they have become integral threads in the tapestry of our lives.

Some of the integral threads in the tapestry of my life have come from a series of conversations I had with Austin Fitts. The first one we had occurred while we were sitting in Hamilton's conference room located above CVS on Dupont Circle in D.C. It was a typical January evening with winter snow in full effect. My interview with Hamilton's HUD Federal Housing Administration (FHA) team had just ended.

"What do you want to do in your career?" Austin asked. Her question felt like an invitation to speak from my heart. So I did. I began sharing how I wanted to integrate my full self into my career by expressing my portfolio of gifts as an artist, finance professional, lawyer, researcher, and writer in a company that affirmed and valued them. I also talked about my desire to work for a company that was committed to social responsibility, invested in technology, promoted teamwork, and provided professional development opportunities for employees. That's when she offered me the position of transaction manager for the FHA team. Before accepting, I asked her why she wanted me to work for her firm. She explained that after talking with her colleague, Wanda Henton, a Lazard Freres investment banker I worked with during my tenure as debt manager, about my success in managing municipal bond transactions and a diverse team of bankers, D.C. government staff, and lawyers, she knew I was the perfect candidate to navigate her firm's $7 billion FHA mortgage sales transaction.

Her next question was about salary. I was not prepared for Austin to ask me how much I wanted. My mind was spinning because I had never been asked to name my salary. I always accepted the employer's offer. Stumbling for an amount, I blurted out my previous salary. Instead of accepting my response as a final number, she encouraged me to think of myself as CEO of my own business and asked me how much I thought I was worth after having served in my former position for two years. Her question helped me formulate what I thought was an acceptable amount. She countered with several thousand dollars more and urged me to always know my value and to confidently demand it.

Everything sounded perfect until I heard my inner voice say, *"Tell her about being fired."* That wasn't a fact I was prepared to reveal because I feared she would decline her offer of employment. Despite my fear, I knew I needed to tell the truth. As soon as I finished explaining the circumstances of my previous employment, Austin shared how she left one job to become an entrepreneur. She told me my value as an employee had automatically increased for having the courage to follow my dreams and travel to China, a country she thought had vast potential for business.

My conversation with Austin taught me several lessons:

- Be authentic and honest.
- Follow your intuition.
- Think of yourself as CEO of your own corporation, ME, Inc.
- Create your career—it's your responsibility.
- Ask for what you want in your career. Don't be afraid
- Know your value.
- Demand what you are worth.
- Live life fully and take what you want from it.

A few weeks after the FHA transaction was completed, I used these lessons to successfully propose a new position as knowledge manager for Hamilton's subsidiary, *e.villages*, an information technology company that provided database services to U.S. Government agencies and the healthcare industry, and hired residents of low-income, underserved communities. During the final salary negotiations, Austin grilled me on why I thought I deserved a significant salary increase. I delivered a confident response that resulted in me gaining a salary that represented what I was worth.

Having Austin as my mentor created tremendous opportunities to learn and grow. Her belief that digital technology and the Internet could be used by entrepreneurs to create new wealth pushed me to be creative in my research, acquire new technology skills, and become a certified Internet geek. She required me to participate in Hamilton's monthly retreats, make presentations at firm meetings, and read magazines like *Fast Company* and books such as Harriet Rubin's *The Princessa*. In addition, she regularly expressed an interest in my writing and art-making. Her efforts inspired me to accept more responsibility including traveling to Istanbul, Turkey to represent the firm and identify new business partners at the U.N. Conference on Human Settlements. They also made me dream of what I truly wanted to do: use my legal training to support Hamilton's business development efforts.

Nine months after I transitioned from the FHA team to *e-villages*, I made a bold move and shared my dream with Austin. She embraced it, outlined Hamilton's current legal needs, and instructed me to develop a proposal to serve as an intellectual property manager of digital products and services. I had no idea what this position would entail, so I quickly reached out to my network and identified attorneys, web sites, and articles. With the help of my research and a newfound friend, Willard A. Stanback, an intellectual property attorney, I designed a blueprint for my dream job and submitted it to Austin. She approved it and made my big dream a reality in January 1997.

When I look back on my Hamilton experiences and the mentoring and sponsorship I received from Austin, I realize I was being prepared to embrace my identity as an Empirista, a woman who thinks of herself as CEO of her own corporation, ME, Inc.; maintains an entrepreneurial mindset; and gives birth to ideas and transforms them into businesses, economies, institutions, networks, and organizations that add value to people's lives.

Writing Exercises: Dream Big

Get a pen and a piece of paper, or turn on your smartphone, iPad, tablet, netbook, laptop, or desktop computer, and reflect on the moments when you have been encouraged and/or mentored by women by answering the questions below.

1. Have you been encouraged to dream bigger and pursue new business or career opportunities by another woman? If so, who encouraged you? What did she say? How did it impact you?
2. Do you have business or career mentors? Who are they? How do they help you grow?
3. Are you an Empirista, a woman who thinks of herself as CEO of her own corporation, ME, Inc.; maintains an entrepreneurial mindset; and gives birth to ideas and transforms them into businesses, economies, institutions, networks, and organizations that add value to people's lives?
4. AlliWorthington.com, Black Business Women Online social networking site, BlogHer.com, ForbesWoman, LittlePINKBook.com, Rise of the Innerpreneur blog, SheTakesontheWorld.com, SuitcaseEntrepreneur.com, TheCRAVECompany.com, TinShingle.com (formerly PRENEUR.net), and WomenGrowBusiness.com are some of my favorite online destinations to visit for information and resources about business and careers. What are your favorite business and career blogs, social networking sites, and web sites?
5. Joining Sarah Massey's Fabulous Women Business Owners DC Meetup was one of the smartest things I have done. The group offers monthly workshops, networking events, a web site with great resources, and an active Facebook group. Are you a part of any Facebook, LinkedIn, or Meetup.com groups that support your business and career?
6. *Black Enterprise*, *Fast Company*, *Inc.*, *More*, and *Wired* magazines are some of my favorite magazines to read for business and career advice. What are yours?

7. Here are a few more ideas—consider them extracurricular activities:

- If you blog, write a post about one or more of your responses above and ask your blog audience to share their comments.

- If you create video, audio blogs, or podcasts, record one about one or more of your responses above. Invite your audience to share their comments on a video, audio blog, or podcast.

- For Facebook, Google+, and LinkedIn users, strike up a conversation with your family, friends, and colleagues by posting a status update about one or more of your responses above. Invite them to share their thoughts.

- For Google Hangout, Skype, UStream.tv, Spreecast, and live stream users, host a live chat about one or more of your responses above. Invite your audience to share their thoughts.

- For Flickr, Instagram, and Pinterest users, post a photo or image that illustrates one or more of your responses above. Encourage your followers to comment.

- Meet a digital sister face-to-face to chat about the discoveries you made while reading this chapter. Use Facebook or Foursquare to check in at your meet up location. Please be careful when you check in. Perhaps you can do the check in when you are leaving the location for safety precautions. Also, be mindful of how much information you share while checking in. Memorialize your meet up with a photo. Consider posting it on Facebook, Flickr, Google+, Instagram, LinkedIn, Pinterest, or Twitter after you have left the meet up location.

- Go a step further and tweet about one or more of your responses above. Invite your Twitter friends to join the conversation. Use the hashtag #empirista. Be sure to send me a tweet about your conversation. I am @anandaleeke and @ digitalsisterhd on Twitter. See you online!

Digital Sisterhood Notes Section

Feel free to use the following pages to write your responses to the chapter exercises, to journal your aha moments, to record golden nuggets of wisdom, or to take notes on whatever pops up in your gorgeous mind! Happy writing!

Digital Sisterhood Notes Section

Ananda Kiamsha Madelyn Leeke

Digital Sisterhood Notes Section

CHAPTER SEVEN

GETTING THROUGH MY DREAM JOB HEARTBREAK

"Owning our story and loving ourselves through that process is the bravest thing that we will ever do." Brene Brown, author of The Gifts of Imperfection, *founder of OrdinaryCourage.com, and research professor*

My heart got broken on an autumn Monday morning as I sat in Hamilton's main conference room with my colleagues. It was October 1997. I was almost 33 years old. My friend, Jill, and I were working together on a community-based transaction in Norfolk, Virginia. With little fanfare, Austin informed us the U.S. Department of Housing and Urban Development cancelled its contract with Hamilton as lead financial advisor to FHA and seized funds owed to Hamilton for work performed. The news made me a casualty and ended my career as an intellectual property manager. It left me with a few hours to wrap up any projects, clean out my desk, say goodbye to colleagues, and return my keys to the human resources department.

As I jumped into survival mode, I kept hearing one of the last things Austin said to me about using what I learned at Hamilton to start a new career and/or become an entrepreneur. That morning, I emailed my network of professional contacts and requested their support in my job search. I also sent myself a series of emails with files of my work product I could use as writing samples for employment searches. By noon, I was back at home sitting in my condo, calling temporary agencies, sending and answering emails, and looking for jobs online. A few days later, I stopped and asked myself what I truly wanted to do. That's when I wrote an action plan describing how I could work as a consultant, artist, writer, and temporary employee.

My plan worked for three months until I exhausted my savings in January 1998. I began relying on financial support from my parents. A few months into the new year, I started to feel the impact of losing my career at Hamilton. Depression set in. Panic attacks followed. I denied it all as I continued to pretend I could handle the loss and move forward. By mid-summer, without a new job, I couldn't fake not feeling the pain any longer. My self-esteem was nonexistent. It was tied to the career I lost. My energy to find consulting work and/or full-time employment was at an all-time low. I could not remember my dreams. Each day I battled internally with myself as my emotions fluctuated between anger and shame. I found it difficult to have hope, practice faith, or believe in prayer.

Things changed when my parents intervened and convinced me to see Carolyn Francis, a licensed therapist and minister at Metropolitan Baptist Church. With Carolyn's support, I started a healing process that helped me surrender my need to control every aspect of my life, confront my loss of employment and career identity, face my depression, understand my need to overachieve, begin to release my shame and guilt, and manage my panic attacks. She gave me homework assignments that encouraged me to use art projects, deep breathing exercises, devotional reading, journaling, meditation, music, poetry, prayer, walks in nature, visits to art galleries and museums, and yoga as healing practices. She also pushed me to acknowledge and accept the choices I made, explore how I could use what I learned to reinvent myself, and develop a plan to secure short-term employment that would offer me the space to explore new career opportunities.

During this time, I started sharing my poetry, favorite inspirational quotes and Biblical verses, and reflections on what I was learning through my healing process with friends via email. It became a weekly exercise that allowed me to release my emotions.

A few friends sent email replies thanking me for inspiring them. My friends, Tanya and "Rosebud" suggested I turn my weekly email into an inspirational newsletter. My therapist Carolyn encouraged me to use the newsletter as a ministry that would draw upon my creative and spiritual practices. And that's how Walk in the Electronic Light Ministry newsletter began.

Working on the newsletter as a ministry gave my life new meaning. It helped me value my creativity as a sacred act. For the first time in my life, I recognized I was more than my academic achievements and career pursuits. As a result, I started to receive invitations to exhibit and sell my artwork which reflected my healing journey. These invitations encouraged me to increase my participation in exhibitions sponsored by the D.C. chapter of the Women's Caucus in the Art, self-publish books of my poetry, and create and sell wire sculpture collections.

A year had passed since I started my first therapy session. It was August 1999. The work I had done with Carolyn helped me reach a new place of peace and acceptance. The more I used my healing practices in my daily life, pursued my creativity, and shared my weekly newsletter, the better I felt. When a new full-time career opportunity presented itself, Carolyn and I discussed how it would help me create financial stability, support my need for therapy, and impact my healing practices, spirituality, creative work, and newsletter writing. This was a new kind of thinking for me that put me on the path to owning my life story and loving all of myself through the process.

Writing Exercises: Your Career Heartbreak

Get a pen and a piece of paper, or turn on your smartphone, iPad, tablet, netbook, laptop, or desktop computer, and reflect on career changes and reinvention by answering the questions below.

1. Have you ever lost a job or career identity? Made a career change that caused you to reinvent yourself? If yes, what happened? How did it impact your emotional, financial, physical, and spiritual well-being?
2. What did you do to cope with the loss or change?
3. What steps did you take to reinvent yourself?
4. What lessons did you learn during the process?
5. Here are a few more ideas—consider them extracurricular activities:

   • If you blog, write a post about one or more of your responses above and ask your blog audience to share their comments.

   • If you create video, audio blogs, or podcasts, record one about one or more of your responses above. Invite your audience to share their comments on a video, audio blog, or podcast.

   • For Facebook, Google+, and LinkedIn users, strike up a conversation with your family, friends, and colleagues by posting a status update about one or more of your responses above. Invite them to share their thoughts.

   • For Google Hangout, Skype, UStream.tv, Spreecast, and live stream users, host a live chat about one or more of your responses above. Invite your audience to share their thoughts.

- For Flickr, Instagram, and Pinterest users, post a photo or image that illustrates one or more of your responses above. Encourage your followers to comment.

- Meet a digital sister face-to-face to chat about the discoveries you made while reading this chapter. Use Facebook or Foursquare to check in at your meet up location. Please be careful when you check in. Perhaps you can do the check in when you are leaving the location for safety precautions. Also, be mindful of how much information you share while checking in. Memorialize your meet up with a photo. Consider posting it on Facebook, Flickr, Google+, Instagram, LinkedIn, Pinterest, or Twitter after you have left the meet up location.

- Go a step further and tweet about one or more of your responses above. Invite your Twitter friends to join the conversation. Use the hashtag #reinvention. Be sure to send me a tweet about your conversation. I am @anandaleeke and @digitalsisterhd on Twitter. See you online!

Digital Sisterhood Notes Section

Feel free to use the following pages to write your responses to the chapter exercises, to journal your aha moments, to record golden nuggets of wisdom, or to take notes on whatever pops up in your gorgeous mind! Happy writing!

Ananda Kiamsha Madelyn Leeke

Digital Sisterhood Notes Section

78

Digital Sisterhood Notes Section

Ananda Kiamsha Madelyn Leeke

Digital Sisterhood Notes Section

I AM
AN
ENCHANTISTA
DIGITAL SISTER!
#dsenchantista

© Leigh Mosley

CHAPTER EIGHT

Y2K Introduces Me to My Enchantista

"You can design a life of creative fulfillment." Gail McMeekin, author of The 12 Secrets of Highly Creative Women

Today, I woke up determined to make it a writing day, but needed inspiration. So I turned on my smartphone and touched the YouTube app. It led me to Owning Pink's Channel, a health and wellness online community established in 2009 by Lissa Rankin, an author and integrated medicine physician. The first time I visited Owning Pink it felt like a virtual feast of empowerment and inspiration. The articles, member blog posts, and discussion forums fed my creative heart and spirit. So I kept returning and eventually signed up for the newsletter and joined the community. Since then, Owning Pink has become a go-to source for healing practices and personal development.

As I scrolled down through the Owning Pink video archive, I located one title that sparked my interest: "Leap Into Your Dreams." The video began with Rankin sharing what happens when your inner critic sets up roadblocks to prevent you from saying "yes" to your dreams. When she shared her own story about taking a leap of faith to start Owning Pink, her vulnerability connected with mine. She reminded me I must trust myself, put my inner critic Broomhilda in a time out, and take a leap of faith because I deserve to have my dreams. Her video was the right dose of digital inspiration I needed to take a leap of faith and begin this chapter. So here it goes.

As much as I thought I wanted to be an artist, writer, and entrepreneur, I had no idea how to manage my finances. I worried all of the time. My fearful emotions distracted me from the things I loved doing: creating wire sculpture art, writing poetry, and working on my first novel. When I started working with my therapist Carolyn in 1998, I realized I did not have the emotional, financial, and spiritual maturity needed to live successfully as a full-time entrepreneur. I also learned financial stability was one of my top three priorities. Gaining clarity helped me release the shame I was carrying about feeling like a failure as a full-time entrepreneur. That release allowed me to work with Carolyn on developing a holistic life blueprint that helped me strengthen myself emotionally, financially, and spiritually.

In 1999, I continued working with Carolyn as I moved forward in my healing journey and full-time employment search. During this process, I worked as a temporary employee and actively pursued my career as an artist and poet with support from the D.C. chapter members of the Women's Caucus for Art. They nourished my creative soul and affirmed my work through group exhibitions, workshops, and invitations to share my poetry at events. Several members mentored me by providing encouragement and counsel on how to increase my revenue streams as a working artist and writer. As a result, I started submitting proposals to local neighborhood women-owned businesses such as Adams National Bank, Lammas Women's Bookstore & More, Sisterspace & Books, and Trade Secrets to exhibit and sell my work. Guess what? They all accepted my proposals and hosted my exhibitions with artist talks.

By the summer of 1999, I had accepted a full-time position with a nonprofit organization that was not as high-pressured as my Hamilton career. It also allowed me financial stability to pursue my creative passion. Through the new job, I learned about the Y2K scare. It was based on the assumption that the world's computer systems would crash on December 31, 1999, because most computers would not be able to distinguish between 2000 and 1900.

As an Internet geek, I breathed in the Y2K scare and allowed it to become a daily fear seasoned with a series of questions. What would happen to all of my newsletters? How would I communicate with my family and friends who lived in different parts of the country and world?

One day I decided to take charge of my Y2K fears. So I asked an information technology colleague for advice. He recommended I get a disk to save my newsletters and emails that were noteworthy. He also urged me to print a hard copy of the documents. I followed his advice and placed the information in folders.

As the new millennium ushered in on January 1, 2000, the world's computers experienced very little inconvenience. Having survived the Y2K scare, my passion for the Internet intensified. I looked for new ways to expand my creativity beyond my Walk in the Electronic Light Ministry newsletter. After reading one of my weekly newsletters, my friend Greg Mays, a former employee of NetNoir.com, wrote me an email inquiring about writing for the site's Gospel and Women's Channels. Accepting Greg's offer was an exciting opportunity because NetNoir.com was as a web pioneer in African American-oriented content and online communities that was launched on AOL in 1995 under the leadership of Malcolm Casselle and E. David Ellington.

In addition, I joined Cheryl Mayberry McKissack's NiaOnline. com, an online community for African American women. I also began learning about the work Shireen Mitchell was doing with Digital Sisters, a D.C. nonprofit organization that was using digital media and technology for women and diverse communities. McKissack and Mitchell's efforts convinced me it was time to carve out my own space in the digital world. So I hired William Jordan of MelaNet, LLC, a firm I worked with while employed at Hamilton, to design Kiamsha.com, my first web site. Kiamsha is a Swahili word I selected as my pen name when I published *My Souls Speaks*, my first chap book of poetry in 1992. It means "that which awakens me." To celebrate the launch of Kiamsha.com, I partnered with the Cyberstop Café, a local Internet café in my neighborhood, to host a web site demonstration that coincided with a book reading for *Feminist Soul 2000*, my collection of poetry and wire sculpture art exhibition that celebrated the authenticity of the human spirit through goddess mythology, in May 2000. What made the event even more special was having my digital sisters "Rosebud" and Tanya present.

Later that summer, my *Feminist Soul 2000* book and wire sculpture collection were featured at Adams National Bank and Lammas Women's Bookstore & More. I gave artist talks and book readings at both locations that included a discussion about the power of the Internet in my creative life and the importance of women claiming their digital space of expression and owning their own web sites to promote their creativity and businesses. After each artist talk and book reading, I collected an email list of the attendees and kept in touch with many of the women who attended the events.

Having their emails expanded my network and opened the door to new opportunities including an invitation to serve as a workshop facilitator for Sacred Circles, a women's spirituality conference sponsored by the Washington National Cathedral in 2001. I drew on my own creative journey in designing my workshop, "Blessed is the fruit of thy womb: Celebrating the Sacredness of Women's Creativity." I published a workbook under the same name that included reflections, meditations, prayers, affirmations, poetry, and writing exercises, and distributed it during the workshop. The feedback I received from Sacred Circles workshop participants included comments about me being a healing artist. Those two words resonated within my soul and felt like they were mine to own. So I claimed them and started referring to myself as a healing artist on my web site and IRL (in real life).

A few weeks later, the Internet geek in me became curious about my new identity as a healing artist. So I did a search online to see what I could find. The first thing I discovered was Smith Center for Healing and the Arts, a D.C. nonprofit health, education, and arts organization, that was located three blocks from where I worked. Excitement danced through my body. I felt like I had hit the jackpot. I emailed Smith Center a short message about my creative journey and desire to learn more about being a healing artist. Shanti Norris, Smith Center's Executive Director, wrote me back and invited me to stop by her office for a chat during my lunch hour. The next day I met Shanti and the conversation we had changed my life. I walked out of her office with an invitation to join Smith Center's new artist-in-residence program that would serve people living with cancer in local hospitals.

That same month, my friend Greg emailed me to inquire about my participation in an article about my journey as an artist in *Heart & Soul*'s October issue. Speechless is the best word to describe how I was feeling. When I calmed down, I accepted the opportunity and began working with Juvita Layne-Abrams, a *Heart & Soul* writer, on the article "Magic Hands." It discussed how I discovered my wire sculpture gifts were inspired by my African ancestors and the creative process I used to make them.

The day I received the October issue in the mail and read my article out loud, I realized my life as a creative professional was fulfilling. It touched every core of my being. It was soulful. It offered ways for me to use my gifts to serve others. It allowed me to inspire and help others heal. It generated revenue for my business. I didn't have the words for it, but looking back I realize I had become an Enchantista, a woman who taps into the magic of her spirit as she focuses her energy, opens her heart, trusts her intuition, embraces her fears, and shares her gifts in service to others.

Writing Exercises: Your Y2K Experiences

Get a pen and a piece of paper, or turn on your smartphone, iPad, tablet, netbook, laptop, or desktop computer, and reflect on life before and after Y2K by answering the questions below.

1. Let's go back to 1999. What did you and/or your family do to prepare for Y2K?
2. How did Y2K impact your online experiences?
3. If you were online in 2000, what web sites did you visit the most? Were you active in any chat rooms or online communities? How so?
4. What are three things you used to do in your digital life in 2000 that you no longer do today? Why have these things changed?
5. Here are a few more ideas—consider them extracurricular activities:

   • If you blog, write a post about one or more of your responses above and ask your blog audience to share their comments.

   • If you create video, audio blogs, or podcasts, record one about one or more of your responses above. Invite your audience to share their comments on a video, audio blog, or podcast.

   • For Facebook, Google+, and LinkedIn users, strike up a conversation with your family, friends, and colleagues by posting a status update about one or more of your responses above. Invite them to share their thoughts.

   • For Google Hangout, Skype, UStream.tv, Spreecast, and live stream users, host a live chat about one or more of your responses above. Invite your audience to share their thoughts.

- For Flickr, Instagram, and Pinterest users, post a photo or image that illustrates one or more of your responses above. Encourage your followers to comment.

- Meet a digital sister face-to-face to chat about the discoveries you made while reading this chapter. Use Facebook or Foursquare to check in at your meet up location. Please be careful when you check in. Perhaps you can do the check in when you are leaving the location for safety precautions. Also, be mindful of how much information you share while checking in. Memorialize your meet up with a photo. Consider posting it on Facebook, Flickr, Google+, Instagram, LinkedIn, Pinterest, or Twitter after you have left the meet up location.

- Go a step further and tweet about one or more of your responses above. Invite your Twitter friends to join the conversation. Use the hashtag #Y2K2000. Be sure to send me a tweet about your conversation. I am @anandaleeke and @ digitalsisterhd on Twitter. See you online!

Digital Sisterhood Notes Section

Feel free to use the following pages to write your responses to the chapter exercises, to journal your aha moments, to record golden nuggets of wisdom, or to take notes on whatever pops up in your gorgeous mind! Happy writing!

Digital Sisterhood Notes Section

Digital Sisterhood Notes Section

Digital Sisterhood Notes Section

PART THREE

FIERCE LIVING 3.0

"Web 2.0 is also the right mix of the social and the technical so that women can prosper. They are contributing in a more visible manner than in other tech fields." Rashmi Sinha, co-founder of SlideShare

"Network weavers provide reasons for people to care about causes and organizations. They shape conversations and identify specific ways for people to help. They inspire people to share a message or idea, donate money, and pass legislation that ultimately makes social change happen." Beth Kanter and Allison H. Fine, authors of The Networked Nonprofit

CHAPTER NINE

BLOGGING SETS MY WRITER SPIRIT FREE

> *"I love blogs, and I also love the concept behind blogs: the juicy meta of this idea that you can represent yourself, your ideas, your work, your thoughts, your art—a random or wild or skillful or free or calculated version of the nexus of artist—person—marketer—public private self in html for the world to jump into like a birdbath, squawking back about what they see."* Deb Rox, *author of* Five Ways to Blank Your Blog

My debut novel, *Love's Troubadours—Karma: Book One* brought me to blogging. Wayne P. Henry, my book editor, suggested I try blogging as a way to overcome my writer's block and to establish a regular writing practice. Wayne thought blogging on a regular basis would help me relax and surrender to the natural flow of my creative process. Desperate, I pushed past my own skepticism.

On February 1, 2005, I posted a poem on my author blog hosted by Blogger.com. In that moment, I knew exactly what Yoani Sanchez, author of *Havana Real: One Woman Fights to Tell the Truth about Cuba Today*, felt when she wrote, "I've only written a few lines, but now I am a blogger." For the first two years, my blog served as a safe haven. I blogged about my writing journey, archived my research for my novel, and shared excerpts from my draft manuscript. Most of my research included articles, quotes, photos, YouTube videos, and links to blogs and web sites related to *Love's Troubadours'* characters and subject matters. They included Afro-Latinos, art, Black men and women, Buddhism, chess, fashion, feminism, historically Black colleges and universities, Haitian art and culture, home décor, Indian culture and history, London, music, museums, online dating, popular culture, spoken word poetry, travel, women's issues, and yoga.

The more I blogged, the freer I felt in my writing practice. After a few weeks of blogging, my goal of developing a consistent writing practice began to manifest. I was able to use parts of my blog posts as dialogue or background in my novel. In addition, I developed a weekly ritual of reading other blogs such as Cathy Delaleu's Lyrically I am Yours, a Haitian-influenced art and poetry blog; and Natalie Lue's Baggage Reclaim, a London-based dating and relationship blog. Each time I visited these blogs, I learned how other bloggers shared their life experiences and interests. They used stories, diary entries, essays, prayers, poetry, photos, podcasts and videos to communicate their authentic voices. I also learned how they interacted with their blog readers through the discussions held in their comment sections.

My blogging life expanded in 2006 when I joined Myspace, a popular social networking site used by a lot of musicians and creative professionals at the time. I used my Myspace blog to cross-post my author blog posts. I also started following people who shared the same interests in art, books, films, music, popular culture, self-care, and spoken word. I read their status updates and blogs, watched their videos, and left comments on their pages. Several people like author and filmmaker Abiola Abrams and Yasmin Coleman, founder of A Place of Our Own Books and Book Club, started following me back and commenting on my page. We developed a social networking relationship that caused them to visit my author blog and leave comments on a regular basis. They also shared my blog links with their network.

After I published *Love's Troubadours* in August 2007, I was able to tap into my author blog and Myspace audience for author interviews and support with my online book party and virtual book tour. Joining Black Author Showcase, a social networking site for African American authors, literary professionals, book clubs, and readers that was established by Diane Williams, Stanford Battle, and Rey O. Harris, gave me valuable information on how to use social media as an author. It broadened my book's audience, exposed me to writing and publishing resources, and introduced me to new social networking sites. I also cross-posted my author blogs, became friends with many members and left comments on their pages, participated in the discussion forums, and shared helpful information and lessons learned from my author journey. As a result of my active participation, I was selected as Member of the Month and was interviewed on Black Author Showcase's Talkshoe.com radio show in February 2008.

Later that year, I began using my author blog as an online journal for my second book, *That Which Awakens Me: A Creative Woman's Poetic Memoir of Self-Discovery*. Many of my blog posts that featured artwork, poetry, reflections, and stories were included in the book. I also started attending blogging conferences like Blogging While Brown, the first international conference for bloggers of color. This experience deepened my understanding of social media, strengthened my online relationships with fellow bloggers, inspired me to explore podcasting and video blogging, and created a network of support for my book launch.

By the time I published *That Which Awakens Me* in 2009, my blogging life had helped me to:

- Identify and sustain my passion for writing books.
- Maintain a regular writing practice.
- Overcome writer's block.
- Communicate and stay connected to my audience which included readers, workshop participants, and creativity coaching clients.
- Create and experiment with content for my books.
- Give back to others by sharing helpful information.
- Promote and market my books and services as a writer, speaker, coach, and workshop facilitator.
- Generate content that could be used in author talks and interviews.
- Obtain interviews and positive media coverage in print and new media.

- Learn about and stay updated on social media and the ways authors use the tools to promote their work and services.

My podcasting and video blogging became the centerpiece of my digital life after *That Which Awakens Me* was published. Although I maintained my author and yoga blogs on a weekly basis, I increased the time I spent communicating with my audience on Facebook, LinkedIn, Ning.com social networking sites, and Twitter. I also began experimenting with several podcasts, live streaming shows on Stickham.com and UStream.tv, and videos about my author journey, creativity coaching, yoga practice, and passion for entrepreneurism, green living, women in social media, and spirituality.

It's been nine years since I entered the blogosphere. My author and yoga blogs have been incorporated into one blog that captures my adventures as a creative professional, yoga teacher, and Internet geek. With the support of an editorial calendar, I write about yoga-inspired topics on Yoga Mondays; social media and technology on Internet Tuesdays; and the arts and creativity on Creativity Thursdays. My passion for fashion, food, fun, and my D.C. lifestyle is expressed on my Tumblr blog, Ananda@16thandU: Lifestylista in Love with DC. With this blog, I don't adhere to a blogging schedule. I do it when I have something to say which means there are times when it goes weeks without an update.

Facebook, Google+, LinkedIn, Pinterest, and Twitter are essential to my blogging life. They serve as my go-to source for audience engagement, content distribution, information sharing, and networking. I also use my email lists, niche communities like BlogHer and SheWrites.com, and StumbleUpon, a web search engine that identifies and recommends content to its users, to share my blogs' content.

I'm still a diehard fan of podcasting, live streaming, and video. Digital photography and photo-sharing sites like Flickr, Instagram, and Pinterest have become my new favorites. I enjoy sharing photos from these sites in my blog posts, tweets, and Facebook status updates.

Maintaining balance in my online life has become a priority. I call it unplugging. In 2012, I discussed some of my unplugging practices during a dialogue I had a panelist at Spelman College's Eighth Annual Leadership and Women of Color Conference in Atlanta, Georgia. My comments described how my early days of blogging laid the foundation for my social media schizophrenia (SMS), the act of owning two or more blogs and managing an active presence on six or more social media sites all at the same time.

Looking back, I now see my SMS began shortly after I launched my online marketing campaign for *Love's Troubadours*. In an effort to spread the news about the book, build an audience for it, and establish relationships with bloggers and social media influencers, I started reading blogs and participating in social networking sites that were related to *Love's Troubadours'* characters and themes. These experiences inspired me to maintain my yoga and author blogs on Blogger.com while launching a women in social media blog on WordPress, four Talkshoe.com radio shows, one BlogTalkRadio show, two niche social networking sites on Ning.com, a video channel on Vimeo and YouTube, three Twitter accounts, three Facebook groups, and two Myspace groups. I kept all of these digital sites active on a weekly or monthly basis. That meant I was always online.

Being online, having so many places to update with content, and reading and making comments on other people's blog posts were major time commitments. It was also exhausting and made me uptight, two facts I couldn't see. It took three years and many conversations with my acupuncturist, attorney, book editor, life coach, PR coach, and yoga teacher, to finally confess I needed to make a change. So I took a blog-cation to recharge myself. When I returned to my blogs, I noticed I did not have the energy or passion to continue writing some of them. That feeling spread to several other social media sites I maintained. Listening to my body also helped me streamline my online presence.

Streamlining my online presence is the greatest blogging gift I have given myself. It has allowed me to enter and exit the blogosphere with ease, grace, and no guilt for the moments when I am unable or unwilling to write a blog post, tweet, or Facebook status update. It has deepened my mindfulness practice and taught me how to take better care of myself.

Writing Exercises: Your Blog

Get a pen and a piece of paper, or turn on your smartphone, iPad, tablet, netbook, laptop, or desktop computer, and reflect on your blog by answering the questions below.

1. Describe the moment you knew and claimed you were a blogger.
2. "You can use your blog as a forum to say whatever you like, or you can start a conversation," writes Margaret Mason in her book, *No One Cares What You Had for Lunch: 100 Ideas for Your Blog*. What are the three most compelling conversations you have started on your blog? How did your blog readers react?
3. Joy Deangdeerlert Cho writes in her book, *Blog Inc.: Blogging for Passion, Profit, and to Create Community*, that "the best thing about being a blogger is having the opportunity to create whatever you want." What do you think is the best thing about being a blogger?
4. "Part of the fun of having a blog is the process of building and maintaining your blog," says Robin Houghton in her book, *Blogging for Creatives*. What lessons have you learned while building and maintaining your blog?
5. Reading books filled with stories about other women's blogging adventures like Tara Frey's *Blogging for Bliss: Crafting Your Own Online Journal: A Guide for Crafters, Artists & Creatives of All Kinds* and Laura Mayes' *Kirtsy Takes A Bow* introduced me to a community of kindred spirits who made me laugh, cry, smile, and reflect in deep silence. Some of these women bloggers wowed me with excitement as they offered insights and tips from the wide wonderful world of women's art, crafts, fashion, fitness, health, home décor, literature, music, photography, and travel. Others gave me life lessons from their world of business, creativity, and technology. As a group, they reminded me how powerful a woman can be when she engages in the act of blogging as a vehicle for self-affirmation, self-expression, and

self-discovery. What are some of your favorite blogging books? How have they influenced your blogging?

6. Have you ever suffered from social media schizophrenia or multiple blog disorder (MBS), a phrase coined by Joy Deangdeelert Cho in her book, *Blogging for Passion, Profit, and to Create Community,* that happens "when we find ourselves starting a new blog because we don't think our newest topic of interest fits the blog we've already established?" How so? What did you do to overcome MBS?

7. Here are a few more ideas—consider them extracurricular activities:

- If you blog, write a post about one or more of your responses above and ask your blog audience to share their comments.

- If you create video, audio blogs, or podcasts, record one about one or more of your responses above. Invite your audience to share their comments on a video, audio blog, or podcast.

- For Facebook, Google+, and LinkedIn users, strike up a conversation with your family, friends, and colleagues by posting a status update about one or more of your responses above. Invite them to share their thoughts.

- For Google Hangout, Skype, UStream.tv, Spreecast, and live stream users, host a live chat about one or more of your responses above. Invite your audience to share their thoughts.

- For Flickr, Instagram, and Pinterest users, post a photo or image that illustrates one or more of your responses above. Encourage your followers to comment.

- Meet a digital sister face-to-face to chat about the discoveries you made while reading this chapter. Use Facebook or Foursquare to check in at your meet up location. Please be careful when you check in. Perhaps you can do the check in when you are leaving the location for safety precautions. Also, be mindful of how much information you share while checking in. Memorialize your meet up with a photo. Consider posting it on Facebook, Flickr, Google+, Instagram, LinkedIn, Pinterest, or Twitter after you have left the meet up location.

- Go a step further and tweet about one or more of your responses above. Invite your Twitter friends to join the conversation. Use the hashtag #yourblog. Be sure to send me a tweet about your conversation. I am @anandaleeke and @ digitalsisterhd on Twitter. See you online!

Digital Sisterhood Notes Section

Feel free to use the following pages to write your responses to the chapter exercises, to journal your aha moments, to record golden nuggets of wisdom, or to take notes on whatever pops up in your gorgeous mind! Happy writing!

Digital Sisterhood Notes Section

Digital Sisterhood Notes Section

Digital Sisterhood Notes Section

CHAPTER TEN

Podcasting Gave My Voice a Platform

"Give voice to what you know to be true." Eve Ensler,
activist, author, playwright, and creator of The Vagina
Monologues

Podcasting is an empowerment tool you can use to give voice to
what you think and care about. It is also a type of digital media that
allows you to create audio content, organize it into an episodic series
of audio files that can be subscribed to and downloaded through
web syndication or streamed online to a computer, laptop, netbook,
tablet, or mobile device when it is convenient to the listener. It
entered my life as a content marketing strategy for my novel, *Love's
Troubadours—Karma: Book One* in 2007.

When I held my first online book party for *Love's Troubadours* on
Myspace, I used my radio experience as a volunteer calendar reader
for WPFW 89.3 FM to develop a podcast series with Gcast, a free
mobile software application. My podcasts featured excerpts from my
novel, reflections about my writing process, and event notices about
book readings and author talks. The more I recorded and posted
podcasts with my cell phone to my author blog and member pages
on various Ning.com social networking sites, the more connected and
engaged I became with my audience.

Through my active participation in Black Author Showcase social
networking site, I learned about Talkshoe.com and BlogTalkRadio,
web-based radio platforms, and was inspired to create two Talkshoe
shows, BAP Living Radio and Go Green Sangha Radio, in 2008.

That same year, I attended a Podcasting 101 workshop taught by Fanshen Cox and Heidi Durrow, the founders of Mixed Chicks Chat, at the Blogging While Brown Conference. The workshop exposed me to Utterli, a mobile micro-blogging tool I began using to post weekly audio blogs about my creative adventures as an artist and author. I also used Utterli to live blog and conduct interviews at events, meet ups, and conferences.

In 2009, Utterli went out of business. That's when I started using BlogTalkRadio and Cinchcast, a micro-blogging tool, to host author chats and to promote my book, *That Which Awakens Me: A Creative Woman's Poetic Memoir of Self-Discovery*. I also launched Digital Sisterhood Radio to document the accomplishments of women in social media and to discuss feminism online. Cinchcast quickly became my favorite podcasting tool because all I had to do was dial a phone number and begin talking into my smartphone to record a podcast.

BlogHer, the premier cross-platform media network that reaches 92 million through its online community and publishing network, invited me to serve as a moderator for the Podcasting 101 Panel with Deborah Shane, author and marketing specialist, and Jasmin Singer, co-founder of Our Hen House, at its annual conference in 2012. Prior to attending the conference, I facilitated two conference calls with Deborah and Jasmin to organize our panel presentation. Based on our discussion, I created a Pinterest Podcasting 101 board of resources. I pinned several of my blog posts that discussed how I used podcasting to:

- Generate conversations through storytelling, sharing information, and interviewing others.
- Create, curate, and market content.
- Advocate and promote causes and campaigns that promote social change, social good, social justice, and other issues.
- Build and engage community.
- Market and promote events, products, and services.
- Develop thought leadership expertise and speaking skills.
- Gather research and document best practices.

The blog posts also discussed my nine benefits of podcasting.

- Podcasting allows you to express your thoughts and opinions as original content with leading edge technology that many people are not using. It helps you stand out among the crowd!
- Podcasting strengthens and highlights your expertise as a thought leader.
- Podcasting helps you develop and demonstrate your skills as a speaker, moderator, panelist, workshop facilitator, and seminar leader for events.
- Podcasting helps you to create a personal connection with listeners by delivering original content in a portable and convenient manner. Because podcasts are like magazines, people can subscribe to them. They can download them to their computers, mobile devices, and mp3 players. Also, people can choose to listen to podcast episodes whenever they want to.
- Podcasting is an easy and cost-effective way for you to market your skills, services, and products. Most podcast platforms are free or inexpensive to use (BlogTalkRadio, VoiceBo, and Talkshoe.com are free for basic services).
- Podcasting helps you cross promote and market your web site, blog, social media sites, products, services, and events.
- Podcasting helps you highlight the work, accomplishments, services, and products of others. Your efforts can create social capital that leads to loyal fans, brand advocates, collaborative partners, colleagues, and sponsors who will support your efforts.
- Podcasting expands your audience for your web site, blog, and social media sites.
- Podcasting helps you build and nurture relationships and networks with listeners who represent potential or existing clients, customers, collaborative partners, donors who contribute to your crowdfunding projects and social good efforts, and sponsors.

One of my blog posts shared my best practices for launching podcasts and Internet radio shows. I was able to share them as tips during the BlogHer Podcasting 101 Panel. They included the following:

- Listen to several podcasts and Internet radio shows to get an idea of how they are organized and hosted.
- Take time to answer the why, what, how, who, and when podcasting questions.
- Why do you want to launch a podcast?
- What themes will your podcast focus on (general themes, episode themes, and guests)?
- How will you host your podcast (podcasting platforms such as BlogTalkRadio, VoiceBo, and Talkshoe.com)?
- Who is your audience (gender, age, ethnicity, geographical location, lifestyle choices, profession etc.)?
- When will you launch your podcast and how often will it air (5 minutes, 15 minutes, 30 minutes, or 1 hour on a daily, weekly, or monthly basis)?
- Create a name for your podcast that supports your brand (blog, web site, social media sites, book, products, and services).
- Select a podcasting platform (BlogTalkRadio, VoiceBo, and Talkshoe.com) that accommodates your schedule, finances, and technical skills.
- Decide if your podcast will include audience participation with questions from a chat room, phone, Twitter, Facebook, etc.
- Determine if you need a digital producer or assistant to help you manage the podcast (introduction, questions in chat room and from guests, live tweeting etc.). Select individuals who are reliable and are able to commit to your schedule.
- Develop an episode schedule with themes, guests, and back up guests. Make sure your themes allow you to provide original content or present content in an original way.

- Spend time making your podcasting site look visually stimulating with your logo or photo and a clear and concise description of the program's themes, episodes, and guests.
- Contact guests well in advance to schedule interviews. Use face-to-face meetings at events, a phone call, Twitter, Facebook, Google+, other social media sites, or email to make the initial contact. Follow up with an email that includes a brief introduction about your show (if they don't know about it), detailed instructions on how to access the podcast, interview questions, additional information about other guests, your contact information, and a request for the guest's contact information (web site, social media sites, and phone number). You may also want to ask the guest for a short bio (200 words or less) and a photo for promotion of the show in a blog post.
- Promote your podcast on your web site, blog, video blog, and social media sites, and wherever your audience hangs out online. Schedule your notices in advance (post a full schedule in advance and monthly or weekly reminders).
- Practice using your podcasting platform several times before your first show. Set up mock interviews with others to practice your interview and hosting skills. Record the shows and listen to them to learn how you can improve your skills. Ask others to listen to the recordings and provide feedback.
- Know that your podcast will evolve over time. So be patient with yourself as you learn and grow.
- Be yourself!
- Have FUN!

Right after I returned home from the BlogHer conference, I received an email informing me Cinchcast was closing its doors. The news left me heartbroken. I felt like I was losing my digital voice. Since then, I have been researching other podcasting platforms. Recently, I discovered VoiceBo, a smartphone app and social networking site that allows you to add your voice to web-based applications or services including Facebook and Twitter. I tried it a few times and have decided it's my new best friend.

Searching for a new podcasting platform reminded me of how technology constantly evolves to meet our needs. Innovative people are always in the lab creating new tools to replace and/or improve the ones we have come to rely on and adore. Our job is to keep our eyes open for the new stuff, try it, determine if it meets our needs, and then use it, knowing full well there will be a new model on the shelves in the morning!

Written Exercises: Your Voice

Get a pen and a piece of paper, or turn on your smartphone, iPad, tablet, netbook, laptop, or desktop computer, and reflect on your voice in the digital space by answering the questions below.

1. Has the digital space helped you develop or strengthen your voice? How so?
2. What podcasting platforms or smartphone apps have you used to express your digital voice?
3. What lessons have you learned from using your digital voice?
4. Here are a few more ideas—consider them extracurricular activities:

    *   If you blog, write a post about one or more of your responses above and ask your blog audience to share their comments.

    *   If you create video or podcasts, record one about one or more of your responses above. Invite your audience to share their comments on a video or podcast.

    *   For Facebook, Google+, and LinkedIn users, strike up a conversation with your family, friends, and colleagues by posting a status update about one or more of your responses above. Invite them to share their thoughts.

    *   For Google Hangout, Skype, UStream.tv, Spreecast, and live stream users, host a live chat about one or more of your responses above. Invite your audience to share their thoughts.

    *   For Flickr, Instagram, and Pinterest users, post a photo or image that illustrates one or more of your responses above. Encourage your followers to comment.

- Meet a digital sister face-to-face to chat about the discoveries you made while reading this chapter. Use Facebook or Foursquare to check in at your meet up location. Please be careful when you check in. Perhaps you can do the check in when you are leaving the location for safety precautions. Also, be mindful of how much information you share while checking in. Memorialize your meet up with a photo. Consider posting it on Facebook, Flickr, Google+, Instagram, LinkedIn, Pinterest, or Twitter after you have left the meet up location.

- Go a step further and tweet about one or more of your responses above. Invite your Twitter friends to join the conversation. Use the hashtag #yourvoice. Be sure to send me a tweet about your conversation. I am @anandaleeke and @ digitalsisterhd on Twitter. See you online!

Digital Sisterhood Notes Section

Feel free to use the following pages to write your responses to the chapter exercises, to journal your aha moments, to record golden nuggets of wisdom, or to take notes on whatever pops up in your gorgeous mind! Happy writing!

Digital Sisterhood Notes Section

Digital Sisterhood Notes Section

Digital Sisterhood Notes Section

CHAPTER ELEVEN

FINDING MY TRIBE OF DIGITAL SISTERS

"The new world of online media, social media, blogs, and virtual communities has brought like-minded women closer together than ever before." *Joanne Bamberger, author of* Mothers of Intention: How Women & Social Media Are Revolutionizing Politics in America

Throughout my online journey, I have discovered my tribe of digital sisters on social networking sites that focus on niche areas, blogs that maintain an active and supportive audience, and at conferences, events, and meet ups.

Finding My Tribe on Social Networking Sites

After I published *Love's Troubadours*, I realized I needed the support of women entrepreneurs who were using the Internet to market and grow their businesses. One of my friends from Black Author Showcase networking site gave me a link to the Black Business Women Online (BBWO), an online network for African-American female entrepreneurs established by LaShanda Henry, an author, web entrepreneur and work-at-home mother.

When Henry launched BBWO, she worked hard to build and encourage a strong sense of community. She made sure the site was filled with an abundance of blogs, discussion forums, groups, and videos that provided information, resources, and training tools to support entrepreneurs at all levels in their businesses. She even added her own e-books including some of my personal favorites, *Black Women Online, Create Your Own Ningalicious Network,* and *Internet Marketing Power.*

Today, BBWO is home to over 9,000 members who are some of the most diverse and successful women entrepreneurs. They are unique because they support other women business owners as they promote their businesses. That means they share advice, connect other women to people in their networks, and purchase each other's products and services. Pam Perry, a PR coach, BlogTalkRadio show host, social media strategist, and chief visionary at Ministry Marketing Solutions, Inc., and Jai Stone, founder of TheBrandCoach. com, are two great examples of BBWO members who give back to the community.

When I started using BBWO on a weekly basis, I read Perry's articles and watched her videos that were packed with information and strategies that helped me to serve as my own publicist and tap into my network for PR support. One of the biggest treats I got was meeting her in person during the 2010 Blogalicious Weekend Conference where she facilitated an informative session on how to use blogs to market your book and build a tribe. Since then, I have faithfully watched her YouTube channel, listened to her BlogTalkRadio show, and read her blog, SlideShare presentations, tweets, and Facebook status updates for additional advice.

Stone's strategies on how build a brand and gain brand recognition through the use of social media were instrumental in helping me identify and express my brand in the digital space. In 2012, I finally had a chance to meet her at the Digitini blogger meet up sponsored by Everywhere, a social media firm, in Atlanta. I was able to personally thank her for helping me develop my brand and business. We reconnected and had a peer mentoring session a few months later during the Shop Your Way "Fashionista" Afternoon Tea at the Blogalicious Weekend Conference in Las Vegas.

Finding My Tribe in Blog Communities

While I was writing my memoir, *That Which Awakens Me*, I discovered Pink Heels, a blog established by Jennifer Moore, a business and career coach and yoga teacher, to empower women to find their passion in their business, career, and lives. Moore's blog was a cozy digital sanctuary that often found me sipping tea as I read blog posts. Each week, her blog featured interviews with inspiring women including artists, authors, branding specialists, business owners, coaches, marketing consultants, tech professionals, and yoga teachers. They offered best practices and wisdom on a variety of topics.

The Pink Heels blog community was very friendly, helpful, open, positive, and welcoming. They were generous with their kind, insightful, and witty comments. They asked and answered questions and offered feedback that included tons of information, life lessons, and resources. That's why it was so easy for me to join in the fun!

Through the Pink Heels community, I met women who became my peer mentors. They included Tara Joyce, communication designer, founder of The Rise of the Innerpreneur blog, and writer; Leah Piken Kolidas, founder of Art Every Day Month, an annual art challenge that encourages bloggers to add more creativity to their daily lives by inviting them to make art and post it on their blogs each day in November, and Creative Every Day blog; Jennifer Lee, author, coach, and founder of Artizen Coaching and Life Unfolds blog; and Jamie Ridler, creative living coach and founder of Jamie Ridler Studios and The Next Chapter, an online book blogging group.

Joyce's Rise of the Innerpreneur blog helped me embrace my identity as an innerpreneur, a person who uses her business to find personal fulfillment and satisfaction through her work. Her blog posts provided resources and tips that guided me in redesigning my business' mission so that it aligned with my personal growth goals. Her monthly profiles introduced me to a community of like-minded innerpreneurs who shared how they were redefining and achieving success on their own terms.

Kolidas' Art Every Day Month (AEDM) challenge was just what the art doctor ordered for me in 2008. I was in the middle of making a collection of artwork for *That Which Awakens Me* and reached a point where I was overthinking my creative process and taking myself way too seriously. My *joie de vivre* in making art was nonexistent. I needed to rediscover my creative play mojo. So I dived deep into Art Every Day Month and abandoned my thinking cap. I purchased a small sketch book, crayons, magic markers, glue sticks, and construction paper from CVS and placed them in my purse so I could create art on the go. I made whatever my heart felt called to create. I stopped judging my process, criticizing my artwork, and proudly took photos of my artwork and posted them on my author blog and the AEDM Flickr group. Each week, I visited the AEDM blog and Flickr group to read about other bloggers' creative experiences. I also left comments on their blogs. They began leaving comments on mine. I noticed how our comments created a kindred bond. By the end of the month, my creative heart was wide open.

Lee used her Life Unfolds blog to express her creative heart's journey from Corporate America to a more authentic life as an artist, author, coach, and entrepreneur. It remains one of my favorite blogs to read. When I first started reading it, I was inspired by how she used her yoga practice and intuitive painting to take better care of herself; reviewed books that gave her golden nuggets of wisdom to share with her blog audience; received guidance and support from her team of advisors, a personal coach, business coach, and mentors; participated in Kolidas' AEDM Challenge and Jamie Ridler's The Next Chapter online book blogging group for community and inspiration; utilized collage techniques to chart her goals and develop a vision of her first book, *The Right Brain Business Plan: A Creative Visual Map for Success*; and shared how she was coping with her book writing process. My connection with Lee was strengthened when we commented on each other's blogs, discussed her creative journey on my Go Green Sangha Radio show, and had dinner at Teaism while she was visiting D.C.

Joining Ridler's The Next Chapter online book blogging group was directly influenced by Lee's earlier participation. Ridler organized the book blogging group by setting up a blog that served as a community gatherings space for women bloggers. They were free to visit, post comments about their experiences and takeaways, ask and respond to questions. The group read a series of creative and self-development books, ranging in topics from creativity to spirituality to money.

The book blogging group was reading *12 Secrets of Highly Creative Women* by Gail McMeekin when I joined in January 2009. At the time, I was in search of a community that could encourage and support me as I finished writing *That Which Awakens Me*. Even though I read McMeekin's book when it was first published in 2000, reading it with the group was more powerful because we were committed to sharing how each chapter impacted us and our creative journey for twelve weeks in a row. Each week when I read the blog posts written by my fellow group members, I learned I was not the only one who experienced a range of highs and lows during the creative process. I also learned how to take better care of myself and nurture my authentic expression.

The next two books that we read included *Wreck This Journal* by Keri Smith, a book that encouraged the spirit of play and silliness in art making, and *The Joy Diet* by Martha Beck, a book that helped me identify, embrace, forgive, listen to, and set healthy boundaries with my inner critic. I continued to use the book blogging group as a source of support during my final editing process for *That Which Awakens Me*.

Finding My Tribe at Conferences

2009 marked the year I witnessed the power of women in social media in real time. It started with an email I received from my digital sister, Jessica Solomon, founder of The Saartjie Project, about the Feminism 2.0 Conference (Fem 2.0). After visiting the Fem 2.0 web site and learning that it was a pro bono project of Turner Strategies that examined the presence and power of women online, and the connection between new media and women's advocacy, I made the decision to attend the conference.

Fem 2.0 conference organizers worked with 14 women's organizations, new media entities, and online networks to produce a one-day conference that took place on February 2, 2009, at George Washington University in D.C. Their efforts gathered over 250 diverse women of African, Asian, European, and Latina descent. It was truly powerful to witness the interaction of every generation of modern womanhood: baby boomers, Gen X, Gen Y, and millennials. Women who defined and embraced their own definition of feminist, womanist, and empowered woman were present. Women who chose not to identify with any labels were also there.

During the conference, I attended the "At the Cross Roads: Organizing the Next Generation of Feminists Online and Off" session. The energy surrounding the conversations in that session reminded me of the conversations I had with women during the UN Conference for Women in 1995. It was inspiring to watch women having a "meeting of minds" across generations and media platforms. I carried this feeling with me throughout the rest of the conference. When I ended my day, I realized I had found a community of sisters and tapped into a powerful network of women online.

A few days later, I visited Fem 2.0's web site and read conference blog recaps written by attendees. Their words inspired me to write "At A Crossroads," a poem about my conference experience.

At A Crossroads

We are at a crossroads.
It is offering us a grand opportunity filled with great awakening.
One that can bring us into a new day that gracefully unfolds into a new tomorrow and future.
It is happening everywhere.
Can you see it?
Can you feel it?
Do you want to be a part of it?

Whether we know it or not, we are manifesting the words of our very own American artist sistalove Meta Vaux Warrick Fuller:

"awakening, gradually unwinding the bandages of [our] past and looking out on life again, expectant but unafraid."

The bandages we are unwinding are complex layers of identities that include our ethnic groups, socioeconomic classes, educational backgrounds, professions, places of residence, sexual orientation, religious affiliation, and political beliefs.

Many of us wear an array of t-shirts that mark us as feminists, womanists, pro-choicers, right to lifers, Democrats, Republicans, green party members, socialists, communists, independents, conservatives, progressives, and middle of the roaders.

Our labels of identity have often created barriers to our growth, coalition-building, understanding, and affirmation as women.

Despite the differences, our identities make us who we are.

They give us individual and collective meaning.

And they must be valued, understood, respected, and affirmed.

With all that said, I am left with a question:

How do we awaken and unwind the bandages from the barriers of the past that created exclusion and misunderstanding?

The answers for those of us who are connecting online reveal themselves a little each day as we interact with social media tools that have the capacity to expand our quilt of sisterhood.

When we tell and document our stories, seek support and advice, educate and train, create and share content, advocate for common causes, launch businesses and nonprofit organizations, market and sell products and services, express our creativity, and engage in dialogue on our audio/video/ text blogs, Twitter, Facebook, MySpace, YouTube, and other social networking and bookmarking sites, we give ourselves the opportunity to learn more about each other.

Our learning efforts can open the door to ways we can honor, promote, and practice diversity, tolerance for a difference of opinion, self-care, compassion, patience, acceptance, mindfulness, loving kindness, and forgiveness.

It all begins with our choice.

If we choose to do the work of understanding who we are and what we believe and want, and seek out common interests without imposing our own strong wills, agendas, beliefs, and branding strategies, we can usher in a much-needed paradigm shift that creates space for our right brain to jump the broom and marry our left brain so that our power, passion, and purpose as women are aligned in strategic ways that give birth to new ways of being, communicating, and working together.

Are we ready to awaken and fully unwind the bandages of our past?

Are we ready to look out on life again, expectant but unafraid of manifesting a shared destiny of common interests while affirming and maintaining our separate identities and causes?

These questions are rhetorical.

We already know the answer.

We are smart, capable, and talented women.

So let's walk past the crossroads and make what we know a reality.
Won't you come?
Won't you come?
Won't you come?

This poem and the Fem 2.0 conference were the catalyst for my decision to increase my participation in social media conferences sponsored by BlogHer, Blogalicious, Latinos in Social Media, and She's Geeky. Each conference experience offered peer networking opportunities that introduced me to amazing women bloggers, entrepreneurs, social media influencers, and new media and technology professionals. Many of these women became my peer mentors when they welcomed me into their communities and generously shared information, insights, resources, tools, and wisdom. Their online and offline work motivated me to create my own tribe, Sisterhood the Blog. I used a WordPress blog, Facebook page, Talkshoe.com podcast, and Twitter account to build sacred space for twenty-first century women to explore self-discovery through sisterhood connections and communities, spirituality, self-care, self-expression, storytelling, social media, and social justice advocacy.

Writing Exercises: Your Digital Sister Tribe

Get a pen and a piece of paper, or turn on your smartphone, iPad, tablet, netbook, laptop, or desktop computer, and reflect on your digital sister tribe by answering the questions below.

1. Name your tribe.
2. Where did you find your tribe?
3. What kinds of activities are you engaged in with your tribe online?
4. What tribe has had the most impact on your life?
5. What have you been able to do as a result of being connected to your tribe?
6. Here are a few more ideas—consider them extracurricular activities:

    - If you blog, write a post about one or more of your responses above and ask your blog audience to share their comments.

    - If you create video or podcasts, record one about one or more of your responses above. Invite your audience to share their comments on a video or podcast.

    - For Facebook, Google+, and LinkedIn users, strike up a conversation with your family, friends, and colleagues by posting a status update about one or more of your responses above. Invite them to share their thoughts.

    - For Google Hangout, Skype, UStream.tv, Spreecast, and live stream users, host a live chat about one or more of your responses above. Invite your audience to share their thoughts.

    - For Flickr, Instagram, and Pinterest users, post a photo or image that one or more of your responses above. Encourage your followers to comment.

Ananda Kiamsha Madelyn Leeke

- Meet a digital sister face-to-face to chat about the discoveries you made while reading this chapter. Use Facebook or Foursquare to check in at your meet up location. Please be careful when you check in. Perhaps you can do the check in when you are leaving the location for safety precautions. Also, be mindful of how much information you share while checking in. Memorialize your meet up with a photo. Consider posting it on Facebook, Flickr, Google+, Instagram, LinkedIn, Pinterest, or Twitter after you have left the meet up location.

- Go a step further and tweet about one or more of your responses above. Invite your Twitter friends to join the conversation. Use the hashtag #dstribe. Be sure to send me a tweet about your conversation. I am @anandaleeke and @ digitalsisterhd on Twitter. See you online!

132

Digital Sisterhood Notes Section

Feel free to use the following pages to write your responses to the chapter exercises, to journal your aha moments, to record golden nuggets of wisdom, or to take notes on whatever pops up in your gorgeous mind! Happy writing!

Digital Sisterhood Notes Section

Digital Sisterhood Notes Section

Digital Sisterhood Notes Section

CHAPTER TWELVE

BLOGHER CONFERENCES ROCKED
MY DIGITAL WORLD

"The story of BlogHer is about a lot of things: it's a narrative about women, blogs, and influence, a story about the rise of social media, and even a commentary on how social technologies are shifting the balance of power in the media industry. But above all, BlogHer portended the wave of women that would flock to social media and technology shortly thereafter." Jessica Faye Carter, author of The Coming Wave: Exploring Women, Innovation, and Social Technology and Double Outsiders

The first time I heard about BlogHer was on Myspace in 2006. One of my Myspace friends posted a link about it. My Internet geek curiosity drew me in and forced me to click on the link. What I discovered was women who flocked to social media and technology to connect and build community for the same reasons I spent time hanging out online with women I met through iVillages in the 1990s and NiaOnline.com and Netnoir.com's Women's Channel in the early 2000s. To be honest, I made that one visit and did not return until two years later.

Here's what happened that brought me back to BlogHer in 2008. While I was attending the first Blogging While Brown conference, I met BlogHer co-founder Elisa Camahort Page. We had several conversations about the BlogHer community and conferences. Page encouraged me to revisit the site and set up a profile page with a short bio and photo. I took her advice and spent my first year in the BlogHer community following the 2008 Presidential election campaign. I enjoyed reading First Lady Michelle Obama's blog posts and other politically inspired posts written by BlogHer members.

My second year was very different. That's when my full blown *blog-affair* with BlogHer began. It was born during the Fem 2.0 conference. I attended a session that featured Page as a panelist. We chatted briefly after the session about the value and benefits of attending the BlogHer conference. Our chat was the reason I registered for the conference a week later.

The BlogHer 2009 conference that was held in Chicago exposed me to a new world of women bloggers. I interviewed many of them with my flip video camera. I visited the Geek Labs and learned new technical skills to support my video blogging, podcasting, and community building strategies for my Talkshoe.com podcast and lifestyle social networking sites on Ning.com. I gained many tips during the sessions that discussed how to own your expertise and transform your blog into a book. I expanded my network through conversations with Deb Rox, author of *Five Ways to Blank Your Blog*, That Black Girl site founder Corynne Corbett, and SheWrites.com founder Kamy Wicoff. These women became peer mentors.

Rox's comments made during a session on transforming your blog into a book lit a fire underneath my creative feet and provided many tips I later used when turning my author blog posts into a creative memoir. After Corbett participated in the Voices of the Year by reading her blog post about First Lady Michelle Obama, she spent time sharing with me how she was using her blog, online community, Internet radio show, social media platforms, and speaking opportunities to build her brand. She also gave me tips on how to develop and improve my brand. While I was sitting next to Wicoff in a session, she pulled out her laptop and gave me a tutorial on how to use SheWrites.com. She also shared blogging and publishing resources, convinced me to become an active member, and encouraged me to host local She Writes meet ups in D.C as a way to build community and network with other women writers. The beautiful thing about these women and the connections we made is that they still exist today!

When it came time to register for the BlogHer 2010 conference, I wasted no time. I headed to New York City for another great experience. I attended the White House Project, a one-day pre-conference seminar, and learned how women could use their online presence to affect political change. Throughout the conference, I used my smartphone and Cinchcast to interview a diverse group of women bloggers I met during sessions. Many agreed to participate in my Talkshoe.com interview series. Right before the conference ended, I met BlogHer co-founder Lisa Stone in the Expo Hall. We talked about the importance of self-care in the blogger community. Stone encouraged me to submit a blogger wellness session proposal for the next conference.

By the time 2010 ended, I submitted my blogger wellness session proposal for the 2011 conference. Having it accepted was one of the things that made BlogHer 2011 mega special. It was also a trip of several firsts. My first trip to San Diego. My first time as a speaker for two sessions, Blogger Wellness and Peer Mentoring. My first time using the BlogHer conference board to find my hotel roommate, Lilian Chang, founder of the Chinese Grandma blog. My first time participating in an unplugging workshop facilitated by Gwen Bell, yoga teacher and author of *Digital Warriorship*.

The BlogHer 2011 conference inspired me to step up my game and submit another series of session proposals for the 2012 conference. Once again, BlogHer selected me to speak. There was a slight twist to the invitation. I was asked to moderate a Podcasting 101 Panel with two digital media rock stars, Jasmin Singer and Deborah Shane. I never would have proposed that topic, however, the BlogHer team saw something I could not see: my thought leadership as a podcaster and Internet radio host.

Incroyable (incredible in French) is the best word to describe BlogHer 2012. First, I was able to see President Obama's live address. Second, I roomed with Arnebya Herndon, founder of What Now and Why blog, who rocked the Voices of the Year when she read her blog post about Trayvon Martin. Third, I gained tremendous insights and inspiration during the luncheon keynotes featuring Katie Couric and Martha Stewart, and the sessions on the brand-blogger connection, how to price and value your services, and travel philanthropy. Fourth, I attended the first-ever BlogHer fashion show that featured women bloggers. Fifth, I had an amazing time celebrating with *mis hermanas* at the Social Fiesta party sponsored by Latinos in Social Media. Sixth, I spoke about the impact the BlogHer and Blogalicious conferences have had on my digital life during the Brunchalicious event.

A few days after I returned home from the conference, I woke up with a deep sense of gratitude for the things the BlogHer team and community have done and continue to do for women. I reflected on how I am a direct beneficiary of their efforts. I smiled at how much I have been able to dream and do as a result of the lessons learned, skills developed, connections I have made, and speaking opportunities I have had. So I wrote an email to the BlogHer co-founders and team members that stated how much I valued what they do to build and nurture its ever-growing and evolving community. I acknowledged how hard it is for them to build a movement, community, business, and economy. I reminded them because they invest in me I invest in them, and we are ONE!

I also wrote a blog post to thank everyone connected to the conference. It included an acronym that offered my understanding of the BlogHer community, conference, and economy.

- *B—Building community through meaningful and mindful connections, conversations, collaborative partnerships and projects, and commerce that generates revenue and valued added exchanges for myself and others.*

- *L—Learning and sharing information that helps me and others grow to our fullest potential.*

- *O—Opening my heart to be inspired and energized by the stories I hear from fellow bloggers, keynote speakers, and representatives from brands, companies, organizations, and marketing/PR firms.*

- *G—Giving back to others by sharing what I know and affirming and supporting others' efforts.*

- *H—Having fun and celebrating digital sisterhood and digital brotherhood bonds with new and old blogging friends.*

- *E—Embracing and valuing the power, presence, and passion of my own voice, creativity, expertise, thought leadership, entrepreneurial efforts, social good causes and campaigns, and definition of success.*

- *R—Remembering that my return on investment (ROI) from my BlogHer community and conference participation is rooted in my attitude, intentions, choices, personal responsibility, and actions.*

I ended the post with these words: *"Together, we are a movement of passionate and powerful people. May we each recognize, affirm, value, and express our contributions in ways that support our highest and greatest good as individuals, communities, businesses, brands, companies, and organizations!"* That says it all until the next BlogHer conference. Hope to see you there!

Writing Exercises: Rocking Your Digital World

Get a pen and a piece of paper, or turn on your smartphone, iPad, tablet, netbook, laptop, or desktop computer, and reflect on experiences that rocked your digital world by answering the questions below.

1. What blogger, social media, or tech conference, meet up or event rocked your digital world?
2. Where did the "rock your digital world" experience take you?
3. What lessons have you learned from the "rock your digital world" experience?
4. Here are a few more ideas—consider them extracurricular activities:

   • If you blog, write a post about one or more of your responses above and ask your blog audience to share their comments.

   • If you create video or podcasts, record one about one or more of your responses above. Invite your audience to share their comments on a video or podcast.

   • For Facebook, Google+, and LinkedIn users, strike up a conversation with your family, friends, and colleagues by posting a status update about one or more of your responses above. Invite them to share their thoughts.

   • For Google Hangout, Skype, UStream.tv, Spreecast, and live stream users, host a live chat about one or more of your responses above. Invite your audience to share their thoughts.

   • For Flickr, Instagram, and Pinterest users, post a photo or image that one or more of your responses above. Encourage your followers to comment.

- Meet a digital sister face-to-face to chat about the discoveries you made while reading this chapter. Use Facebook or Foursquare to check in at your meet up location. Please be careful when you check in. Perhaps you can do the check in when you are leaving the location for safety precautions. Also, be mindful of how much information you share while checking in. Memorialize your meet up with a photo. Consider posting it on Facebook, Flickr, Google+, Instagram, LinkedIn, Pinterest, or Twitter after you have left the meet up location.

- Go a step further and tweet about one or more of your responses above. Invite your Twitter friends to join the conversation. Use the hashtag #rockyrdigitalworld. Be sure to send me a tweet about your conversation. I am @anandaleeke and @digitalsisterhd on Twitter. See you online!

Digital Sisterhood Notes Section

Feel free to use the following pages to write your responses to the chapter exercises, to journal your aha moments, to record golden nuggets of wisdom, or to take notes on whatever pops up in your gorgeous mind! Happy writing!

Digital Sisterhood Notes Section

Ananda Kiamsha Madelyn Leeke

Digital Sisterhood Notes Section

146

Digital Sisterhood Notes Section

© Leigh Mosley

CHAPTER THIRTEEN

Making It Personal
with Blogalicious' Passion

"Being Blogalicious means to be genuinely passionate about your relationships, your work and your passions, rooted in social media, and to live that passion." Stacey Ferguson a/k/a Justice Fergie, Blogalicious co-founder and chief curator

Something spectacular in the world of social media happened on October 9-11, 2009, in Atlanta, Georgia. It was the Blogalicious Weekend, the inaugural conference created to celebrate diversity in the blogosphere. The conference attracted women bloggers of color and other interested women and men.

The W.O.W. Factor

The 2009 conference theme was "Your WOW Factor" which referred to the unique qualities that distinguish each woman blogger in the social media market. In a post conference article I wrote for my Examiner.com column, I transformed WOW into an acronym:

"*Women Owning Who* they are through the content, connections, communities, and commerce they create as they share experiences, insights, opinions, humor, creativity, expertise, and information. In short, they represent 21st century sisterhood."

The conference kicked off with a Friday night of fun that included a welcome cocktail reception sponsored by "So In Style" by Barbie and Pine Sol. During the reception, I had an opportunity to meet and chat with the Migdalia Rivera of Ms. Latina blog, Nirasha Jaganath of Mommy Niri, Yakini Etheridge of The Prissy Mommy Chronicles blog, Renee Ross of Cutie Booty Cakes blog, Thien Kim of I'm Not the Nanny blog, and PR professional Xina Eiland. Chatting with these women helped me quickly recognize that Blogalicious was more than a conference. It was a movement comprised of a bold new breed of brilliant and beautifully different women bloggers.

The next two days of the conference were spent attending sessions that discussed social media basics, taking your blog to the next level, the possibilities and pitfalls of being on the Internet, the art of small business blogging, marketing to women of color, hot social media trends, secrets to a successful blog, and blog-life balance. I was able to teach an office yoga session for social media users. The feedback I received from several attendees including Boni Candelario of CoachMUp.com encouraged me to approach Maria Bailey, founder of MomTV, about hosting a yoga class on her online network, during the conference. She welcomed my proposal and later approved it for launch a month after the conference.

Throughout the conference, I used my flip video camera to conduct interviews with women bloggers and speakers including my digital diva shero, Cheryl Mayberry McKissack, founder of NiaOnline.com. When I returned home, I posted the videos on my YouTube channel and shared them with the Blogalicious community on Facebook and Twitter. I also launched a Blogalicious interview series on my Sisterhood the Blog radio show that featured many of the conference attendees and speakers. These efforts helped me give back to and truly embrace the Blogalicious community as my own.

Making It Personal

During the opening reception, I spent a lot of time sipping cocktails and chatting with Xina. We learned we were both born in Michigan and currently living in the D.C. metropolitan area. Throughout the conference, we reconnected with each other and other women like "WhimsiGal," founder of Whimsicard, LLC from the D.C. area. When we returned home, we used Facebook, LinkedIn, and Twitter to stay in touch. We also discussed our Blogalicious experiences on my Sisterhood the Blog radio show.

And then it happened. We reached out by telephone and agreed to meet face-to-face in D.C. Our first meeting occurred on a Sunday afternoon at the U Street Café in December 2009. Xina, "WhimsiGal," and I sat at a table for a few hours discussing our lives, life goals, ways we could support each other, and ideas for a local Blogalicious meet up. That one conversation paved the way for our Blogalicious D.C. community building efforts.

Together, we were able to help Blogalicious co-founder Stacey Ferguson organize two D.C. meet ups in February and April 2010. Xina played a major role in securing space and media coverage, promoting the events on Facebook and Twitter, identifying speakers and sponsors, developing the agenda, and obtaining in-kind donations for both events. I served as panel moderator for the April meet up.

In addition to supporting the Blogalicious D.C. community, we also made a commitment to support each other and our business goals as accountability partners and peer mentors. We launched our commitment with a breakfast meeting at Busboys and Poets, a popular D.C. hangout, in January 2010. Seated on comfy chairs with herbal tea and delicious breakfast items to keep us company, we shared our expertise. Xina became my PR coach. She convinced me to follow her instructions on branding for my books, artwork, yoga practice, speaking and sponsorship opportunities, and coaching services. I became her creativity coach and helped her develop a social media plan to support her intention to blog and learn more about social media tools.

Throughout 2010, we met monthly to assess our progress and seek feedback. We attended several D.C. social media meet ups, participated in the Blogging While Brown's White House Visit and weekend conference, hung out at the Red Pump Project and Blogalicious' Say RED: Cocktails and Conversations event, and live blogged with the Blogalicious D.C. B-Link members during President Obama's education reform speech at the National Urban League's Centennial Conference. We also traveled to Miami to attend Blogalicious' second annual conference. Xina served as the conference publicist. Together, we served as co-moderators of an open-mic luncheon sponsored by McDonald's.

Our open-mic luncheon discussion was soulful and filled with personal testimonies and stories shared by women who were Blogalicious newbies and alumni. They opened their hearts and spoke with such passion, clarity, candor, and humor. Their collective energy made it a beautiful experience filled with wisdom, laughter, lessons learned, and a plethora of blogging experiences that revealed how women discovered their authentic selves and voices online and offline through the support of other women.

In 2011 and 2012, Xina and I continued to serve the Blogalicious community by promoting and participating in the annual conferences, meet ups, and Twitter chats. As a result of Xina's PR efforts, she became the Blogalicious Publicity Director. I became a blogger ambassador, a conference speaker, and a media partner. When I look back on our experiences, I realize our connection is one of my life's greatest blessings. Here's why. We always encourage each other to step up our game and pursue new opportunities. We share information, insights, and introductions to people in our network that can support our efforts. We laugh, learn, and listen to each other when we achieve and struggle. We are great event planning partners, travel buddies, and conference roommates. We make sure we attend and participate in a wide range of business and social media events. Over the past five years, I think we have succeeded in making our Blogalicious experience personal by cultivating a strong bond of friendship that is deeply rooted in the Blogalicious passion and sisterhood.

<u>Blogalicious</u>

A poem that celebrates the fifth anniversary of the Blogalicous Weekend Conference

Magic happens when we come together in the digital space.

It's powerful. It's passionate.

It's creative. It's collaborative.

It's beautiful and brilliant all at the same time.

This electrifying energy travels inside each of us at light speed, expanding exponentially when we come face-to-face.

It calls us to express our authentic voices and embrace our unique identities.

It gives birth to and celebrates a diverse community.

It connects us to one another and offers bonds of friendship that affirm and nourish our dreams.

It manifests as partnerships that promote social good and generate revenue streams.

It forces us to move beyond our comfort zones even when we feel we are not ready.

We lean on each other and ask for support.

Our confidence and faith in what is possible grows beyond what we know.

Our ears open to listen and our hearts discover wisdom for what is coming next.

The guidance we receive helps us to find the resources we need.

Before you know it, we are busy creating, building, and funding our dreams.

Writing Exercises:
Making Your Experiences Personal

Get a pen and a piece of paper, or turn on your smartphone, iPad, tablet, netbook, laptop, or desktop computer, and reflect on how you make your experiences at conferences and events personal by answering the questions below.

1. I am a natural born connector who loves to build community. Whenever I attend conferences and events, I develop a list of outcomes I am seeking to attain and relationships that would make the experience meaningful. I review the agenda and select sessions, parties, and off-site events to attend; speaker bios; and the list of sponsors and participants. This information helps me create a conference or event Twitter list. I also follow the conference or event hashtag and participate in Twitter and Facebook chats with attendees, speakers, and sponsors. Reading pre-conference or event blog posts is also informative. How do you prepare before attending conferences and events?

2. When I arrive at the conference or event, I commit to connecting with and having a focused conversation with three to five new people. During those interactions, I make certain to listen fully to what people are saying. I ask several follow up questions based on what the individual has shared. On many occasions, I invite the individual to take a photo with me and participate in a podcast or video interview. If they are not interested, I ask if I can interview them on Digital Sisterhood Radio or send them a blog interview request via email that would allow them to respond to written questions and be featured on my blog. How do you connect with people you meet or know at conferences and events?

3. What would strengthen your ability to make your conference and event experiences more personal and meaningful?

4. Here are a few more ideas—consider them extracurricular activities:

- If you blog, write a post about one or more of your responses above and ask your blog audience to share their comments.

- If you create video or podcasts, record one about one or more of your responses above. Invite your audience to share their comments on a video or podcast.

- For Facebook, Google+, and LinkedIn users, strike up a conversation with your family, friends, and colleagues by posting a status update about one or more of your responses above. Invite them to share their thoughts.

- For Google Hangout, Skype, UStream.tv, Spreecast, and live stream users, host a live chat about one or more of your responses above. Invite your audience to share their thoughts.

- For Flickr, Instagram, and Pinterest users, post a photo or image that illustrates one or more of your responses above. Encourage your followers to comment.

- Meet a digital sister face-to-face to chat about the discoveries you made while reading this chapter. Use Facebook or Foursquare to check in at your meet up location. Please be careful when you check in. Perhaps you can do the check in when you are leaving the location for safety precautions. Also, be mindful of how much information you share while checking in. Memorialize your meet up with a photo. Consider posting it on Facebook, Flickr, Google+, Instagram, LinkedIn, Pinterest, or Twitter after you have left the meet up location.

- Go a step further and tweet about one or more of your responses above. Invite your Twitter friends to join the conversation. Use the hashtag #makeyrexperience. Be sure to send me a tweet about your conversation. I am @anandaleeke and @digitalsisterhd on Twitter. See you online!

Digital Sisterhood Notes Section

Feel free to use the following pages to write your responses to the chapter exercises, to journal your aha moments, to record golden nuggets of wisdom, or to take notes on whatever pops up in your gorgeous mind! Happy writing!

Ananda Kiamsha Madelyn Leeke

Digital Sisterhood Notes Section

Digital Sisterhood Notes Section

Digital Sisterhood Notes Section

© Leigh Mosley

CHAPTER FOURTEEN

EMPOWERISTA DECLARES
HER DIGITAL SISTERHOOD MANIFESTO

"A manifesto is a bold and powerful public declaration of what you stand for. It's a catalyst to step up to the platform of your innermost truth. It's a call to action of how you want to sculpt your words and efforts for the betterment of humankind." Sianna C. Sherman, founder of ManifestoMovement.com, poet, and yoga teacher

Right after the Blogalicious Weekend ended in 2010, I sat with my PR coach Xina eating lunch and chatting about our conference takeaways in the poolside café at the Four Seasons Hotel Miami. One of my greatest takeaways was interviewing conference attendees about their definition of digital sisterhood and realizing how much they embraced, identified with, and adored the phrase. The other takeaway was learning how Twitter conversations that use hashtags and are scheduled on a weekly basis help build community, influence, and relationships during a keynote presentation given by James Andrews, founder of SocialPeople.tv.

I told Xina how Andrews' presentation convinced me to launch #DigitalSisterhood Wednesday, a weekly Twitter celebration that would use the Friday Follow format to give women in social media an opportunity to build and strengthen their communities. She suggested I make a video about it. So I gave her my camera and we spontaneously recorded a short video that invited women to participate in #DigitalSisterhood Wednesday by tweeting other women and sharing information about their blogs, businesses, campaigns, causes, creativity, dreams, expertise, experiences, events, lessons learned, and links to social media and web sites. The next day I reserved and paid for Digital Sisterhood's domain name and registered it on Twitter. My Sisterhood the Blog web site and radio show were renamed to reflect this change.

October 13, 2010, marked the launch of the first #DigitalSisterhood Wednesday Twitter celebration. I had no idea if women would embrace it. It was something bigger than me. It felt like I was called to do it. So I stepped up and did it without a real plan or expectation for what would come next. It was organic and fluid. Something directed from my innermost truth. And then it happened. My Blogalicious sisters jumped on board and began tweeting and retweeting each other. They breathed life into what my intuition was guiding me to do.

What is Digital Sisterhood?

As the weeks passed by and more women participated in the Twitter celebrations, I began to journal about the meaning of digital sisterhood. I reread blog posts I wrote and notes I made about conferences, events, and meet ups I attended. I watched video interviews and listened to podcasts and radio interviews featuring women bloggers I met. The end result was a statement that echoed my feelings about the power of women in the digital age:

> *Digital sisterhood is the feminine currency women use to create relationship wealth through the connections they make, conversations they have, communities they build, causes they support, collaborative partnerships they establish, and commerce they engage in with women they meet online and offline. The relationship wealth of digital sisterhood is based on what women care about and their shared interests and experiences. This wealth supports women as they stand in their*

own power and reclaim themselves online and offline. When they do so, they move with a power not seen before. It is rooted in women being fully,

P—Present when they
O—Own their lives as
W—Women who believe they have
E—Everything they need to live out their
R—Revolution of authenticity.

When all women know their investment in themselves and each other, they will yield a high return!

This statement became my manifesto, a catalyst for me to embrace my calling: celebrating women in social media. It also transformed me into an Empowerista, a woman who creates and curates content, shares information and experiences, connects with others and establishes positive relationships, and builds and participates in communities that empower her and others.

Digital Sisterhood Month

Digital Sisterhood Month developed as a result of women asking me what I was going to do next with the #DigitalSisterhood Wednesday Twitter celebrations. I didn't have an immediate response and was not looking to develop another project. However, my intuition stepped in once again and whispered, *"host a month-long celebration that women can participate in annually."* I tried to ignore my inner voice, but it kept getting louder. Just when I was ready to run for the hills, my inner voice reminded me of my manifesto. I took a deep breath, did some yoga, gave myself some Reiki healing touch, sat in meditation, and said a prayer of surrender.

Guidance on what to do began to sprinkle itself into my daily activities. It helped me develop a schedule of online events including blog posts, Digital Sisterhood Radio interviews with women thought leaders, suggestions on how women could celebrate with their online and offline networks, Twitter chats for #DigitalSisterhood Wednesdays, giveaways, and online yoga classes. Offline events for D.C. area women including a writers' meet up at a woman-owned tea café, field trip to the National Museum of Women in the Arts, and yoga class field trips to woman-owned studios were held. In addition, Shameeka Ayers, an African American woman, wife, mother, and Chief Lifestyle Officer of The Broke Socialite, was selected as the Digital Sister of the Year because of her achievements and community building efforts as a blogger, entrepreneur, and founder of lavish!, the first unconference for lifestyle social networkers.

Logo Created by Dariela Cruz

Digital Sisterhood Network

One of the most popular questions I received during the first Digital Sisterhood Month celebration centered on my plans for 2011. I honestly didn't have any until I realized how appreciative women in the digital space were for Digital Sisterhood Month. So I said another prayer of surrender and waited for my guidance. When it came, it showed up as the Digital Sisterhood Network (DSN), a media channel that promotes digital sisterhood as a self-care, self-discovery, and social justice movement for women in social media. Once again, I had no idea what this meant or entailed. I followed my intuition and went with the flow of the year which produced a series of initiatives.

She Writers Meet Up

DSN partnered with SheWrites.com, a social networking site for women writers, to sponsor a series of quarterly meet ups for D.C. area women writers. The first meet up celebrated SheWrites.com's first year anniversary at Teaism, a woman-owned tea café. It attracted an intergenerational group of women who discussed their favorite writers, current work, and challenges. Subsequent meet ups offered the group opportunities to network, discuss writing projects, and listen to guest writers read from their new books.

Blogger-in-Residence Program

DSN established a year-long blogger mentoring program to serve a woman living in the D.C. area. Kamaria T. Richmond, an African American writer living with sarcoidosis and recovering from a stroke, was selected to participate in the program. During the mentoring program, Richmond learned how to use social media tools and strengthen her voice online. The experience helped her explore and express her passions and interests, cultivate her own network of social media colleagues, exposed her to local and online social media events, and develop and implement long-term strategies to support her life reinvention. She created audio blog posts, developed and hosted The Stroke Diva Fabulous Show on Digital Sisterhood Radio, and attended meet ups and the Blogalicious Weekend Conference.

Digital Sisterhood Unplugged Sundays

DSN utilized Digital Sisterhood Unplugged Sundays to encourage women to step away from their tech devices and to-do lists, unplug each month for an hour, half-day, full-day, weekend, week, or longer so they could take a break and recharge themselves. In 2013, the event expanded to an entire weekend. Blogs posts with tips and resources including articles and blogs on how to unplug, go on a digital diet, take digital sabbaticals, and develop a digital wellness plan were published.

2011 Digital Sisters of the Year

Stacey Milbern and Mia Mingus were named the 2011 Digital Sisters of the Year. Milbern and Mingus are queer disabled diasporic Korean women of color who moved from the South to the San Francisco Bay area to create home and community with each other. They launched their To The Other Side of Dreaming blog as an experiential project that documented their journey to create collective access and home through letters and videos. Their stories and life work touch the core of humanity's heart. They remind us how powerful women are when they connect and cultivate friendships, engage in conversations, build community, establish collaborative partnerships, and support social justice causes based on shared interests.

Feminism Online Project

Feminism is many things to many people. It lives out loud in the arts, environment, holistic health field, media, music, popular culture, and spirituality. It is woven into the fabric of individuals' beliefs and life practices. It makes its home in diverse communities. It explores its theories in the halls of academia. It tests its application and elasticity in businesses, governments, and institutions. It invites comment and critique wherever it goes. It seeks to bridge the gap between its first, second, third, fourth, and fifth waves. It comes online and dances with complexity backed up by a rainbow chorus of voices, some of which go unheard. DSN created an acronym to define feminism and the Feminism Online Project:

- F—Freedom of choice that encompasses a movement, practices, and beliefs that promote social, political, and economic equality and
- E—Empower women, girls, men, and boys to
- M—Move through their daily lives, the Internet, and society as
- I—Individuals who are treated as equals and
- N—Nurtured and respected for the diversity of their
- I—Identities as human beings who

- S—Share the responsibility of
- M—Making their daily and digital lives, communities, organizations, businesses, governments, countries, and societies' oppression-free zones.

The Project celebrated the diverse feminist voices in the digital world through blog posts, Digital Sisterhood Radio interviews, and Twitter chats from March 2011 to May 2011. These efforts helped to documented how the Internet has democratized feminism in ways that no other vehicle has in the past. As a result, the Internet has become a convenient mobilizer space that can quickly organize people into coalitions and launch campaigns that advocate for and against political and social policies. It has made feminism available and accessible to a diverse audience of women who live in different geographical locations around the globe, especially women of color, disabled women, women from different socioeconomic classes and religious groups, and women who self-identify as lesbian, bisexual, transgender, and queer.

These women have been able to build web-based platforms of self-expression with their blogs, social media, and visual content that tell their stories, share and affirm their experiences, develop thought leadership, and promote advocacy, political, and social good campaigns. Their presence has created a multi-vocal feminism that represents and bridges the gap between the academy, activists, and everyday people who support women's empowerment. Their voices create greater accountability.

ERA 2015 Awareness Campaign

DSN partnered with Carolyn Cook, founder of United 4 Equality, LLC, a D.C. based grassroots coalition of citizens, nonprofit organizations, and corporations committed to outlaw sex discrimination, on the Equal Rights Amendment (ERA), to launch the ERA 2015 Awareness Campaign on #DigitalSisterhood Wednesdays in June 2011. Each Wednesday, DSN tweeted about the importance of the ERA and United 4 Equality's ERA 2015 Campaign.

Digital Civility & Security Initiative

Technology, the Internet, and social media have empowered people with information, a global space, and a portfolio of tools to communicate, to promote, and to debate their ideas and experiences. They have also presented challenges in how people communicate and engage with each other as they exercise their freedom of speech on blogs, Facebook, Twitter, YouTube, and other sites in cyberspace. Some of these challenges include speech that causes fear or creates a threat of being the target of unwarranted abuse, harassment, or lies. Thanks to organizations like CiviliNation, an education and research nonprofit that focuses on advancing the full capability of individuals to communicate and to engage in cyberspace in a responsible and accountable way, work is being done to educate people about these challenges.

In an effort to support CiviliNation's work and to promote digital civility, DSN launched its Digital Civility & Security Initiative which was held from July 4 to July 11, 2011. It used blog web site and #DigitalSisterhood Wednesday Twitter celebrations to promote women and organizations that conduct awareness and outreach on digital civility, Internet freedom of speech, online security, privacy, cyber bullying, digital drama, and digital etiquette. It addressed cyber-violence and cyber-stalking against women. In addition, Andrea Weckerle, CiviliNation's founder, co-hosted a Twitter chat on digital civility.

Digital Sisterhood Month 2011

"Celebrate the 4Fs of Women's Health: Feelings, Food, Fitness & Fierce Living" was the theme of Digital Sisterhood Month 2011. Everywhere, Shootie Girl, and Susan G. Komen for the Cure served as sponsors. The month-long celebration kicked off with the Fierce Living Campaign on Facebook and Twitter. The campaign featured daily posts that honored women who use their social media presence to build community for women; empower and inform women and girls; coach and inspire women to feel and think positively, dream big, and live full lives; promote fitness, healthy eating, and healthy living; and share how their health journeys have helped them reinvent their lives. Twitter chats and giveaways, Digital Sisterhood Radio interviews, and online yoga classes were held. Women bloggers participated in guest blog interviews on the DSN blog. D.C. area women attended a breakfast meet up at Teaism, "Fierce Living in Fashion" Tweetup at Violet Boutique, field trip to the National Museum of Women in the Arts, She Writers meet up at Teaism, and yoga field trips to Embrace and Tranquil Space yoga studios.

Leadership Project

In her 2011 Digital Women: from geeks to mainstream presentation that was given at the WIFT International Women Conference for Digital Women, Dr. Taly Weiss, a social psychologist and CEO/Founder of Trendspotting, concluded that "women are dominant digital users . . . they breathe and live digital." Dr. Weiss' conclusion caused me to explore how women have become Digital Sisterhood Leaders, ambassadors of social expression who share what they are passionate about online. My exploration revealed they use their social media platforms to:

- Advocate for causes.
- Build communities.
- Create mobile applications, art, books, businesses, products, publications, services, tools, and webisodes.
- Curate content.
- Educate and inform.
- Give voice to their thoughts as subject matter experts, thought leaders, and brand ambassadors.
- Share information and experiences.
- Explore and experiment with new technologies as early adopters and trendsetters; to engage in social good.
- Influence others with their lifestyles and personal interests.
- Inspire and motivate.
- Mentor.
- Network.
- Tell their personal stories.

- Promote and celebrate the expertise, gifts, and talents of others.

Based on their online activities, I identified 12 key leadership roles they play: advocate, community builder, creator, curator, educator, influencer, mentor, motivator, promoter, social do gooder, storyteller, and thought leader.

My participation in Spelman College's Leadership & Women of Color Conference and the information I read about while visiting web sites and social media maintained by The Hot Mommas Project at George Washington University School of Business, Barnard College's Athena Center for Leadership Studies, and Simmons College inspired me to establish the Digital Sisterhood Leadership Project (#DSLead) in May 2012. #DSLead explores, documents, and celebrates the creative ways women express their leadership abilities and experiences online and offline.

#DSLead Project's soft launch began with a Digital Sisterhood Radio interview with Dana Theus, founder of InPower Women, that focused on the leadership roles social media women play and tips on how to establish a personal leadership brand with social media. The soft launch also included Twitter chats that discussed women's social media leadership, how social media women develop their personal leadership brands, social media women as community builders, and social media women as social good leaders.

Leadership, Lifestyle, and Living Well Initiative

Throughout 2012, the #DSLead Project featured a series of interviews with women leaders on the DSN blog. They inspired me to expand its scope to include lifestyle and wellness issues through the Leadership, Lifestyle, and Living Well initiative. DSN announced the Initiative's first program activity, the American Association of Retired Persons (AARP) Blogger Kitchen Cabinet #CareSupport Campaign in November 2012. It honored women caregivers during National Family Caregivers Month by promoting awareness of AARP's Caregiving Resource Center, sharing caregiving stories, and offering tips to help women take better care of themselves and their loved ones.

The second program activity was a blogger ambassador partnership with Maiden Nation, a company and social platform that empowers women activists, artists, and entrepreneurs around the globe through ethical fashion. Under the leadership of Willa Shalit, a social entrepreneur and the founder of Fairwinds Trading, Maiden Nation offers an online marketplace featuring unique, handcrafted pieces designed by Maiden designers. It also provides Maiden activists and citizens of a digital community to share their ideas, goals, and causes.

In an effort to celebrate the Digital Sisterhood Month 2012 theme, "Creativity + Great Health = Fierce Living Women," DSN promoted Maiden Nation's efforts during #DigitalSisterhood Wednesday celebrations. It also sponsored a series of lifestyle and living well events in D.C. including a field trip to U Street boutiques for fashion and style bloggers and enthusiasts that used the "cash mob" model of supporting local businesses created by CashMob.com; a D.C. Style Salon Series featuring a fashion and style bloggers' town hall at a local library; a Twitter chat for beauty, fashion, lifestyle, and style bloggers; a "Sweet Treats: Coffee, Tea and Dessert" meet up for women bloggers and social media influencers at the Mediterranean Spot; a She Writers meet up at Teaism; a field trip to see the "Women Who Rock: Vision, Passion, and Power" exhibition at the National Museum for Women in the Arts; and yoga class field trips to Embrace and Tranquil Space yoga studios. Two events were held in New York City: a "Drop By and Chat" meet up at Argo Tea and a field trip to see the "Mickalene Thomas: Origin of the Universe" exhibition at the Brooklyn Museum.

DSN named a diverse group of 100 women as the 2012 Digital Sisters of the Year a/k/a the Digital Sisterhood 100. They included Veronica Arreola, founder of Viva La Feminista blog; Gwen Bell, global entrepreneur and yoga teacher; Kimberly Bryant, engineer and founder of BlackGirlsCode.com; Ana Roca Castro, founder of Latinos in Social Media; Elisa Camahort Page, BlogHer co-founder; Lilian Chang, founder of ChineseGrandma.com; Dr. Ayoka Chenzira, digital media artist and Spelman College's Digital Moving Image Salon; Stacey Ferguson, Blogalicious co-founder; Jory Des Jardins, BlogHer co-founder; Stephanie Piche, founder of Mingle Media TV; Issa Rae, founder of "The Misadventures of Awkward Black Girl" webisode series; Shivani Sopory, co-founder of Women 2.0; Lisa Stone, co-founder of BlogHer; Zeenat Merchant-Syal, founder of PositiveProvocations.com and psychologist; Dr. Beverly Daniel Tatum, President of Spelman College; and Deb Vaughn, founder of Real Girl Runway blog. See the Appendices for a complete list.

2013 and Beyond

I will continue to follow my manifesto and listen to my intuition for guidance on how to grow DSN as it uses its blog, radio show, social media sites, and events to explore women's entrepreneurship, crowdfunding efforts, healthy lifestyle, leadership, and software development. You are cordially invited to watch and get involved as it unfolds organically!

Writing Exercises: Your Manifesto

Get a pen and a piece of paper, or turn on your smartphone, iPad, tablet, netbook, laptop, or desktop computer, and reflect on your manifesto by answering the questions below.

1. Do you have a manifesto for what you stand for online? If so, write it down. If not, sit quietly (10 to 15 minutes) and reflect on what you stand for online. When you finish, make a list of the key words that you thought about during your quiet time (10 to 15 minutes). Review the list and use the key words to describe what you are seeking to achieve through your digital presence and interactions (20 to 30 minutes).

2. How do you currently express or plan to express your manifesto in the digital world?

3. What Digital Sisterhood Network initiatives reflect your manifesto?

4. Consider organizing a meet up or events for digital sisters in your local community like the ones mentioned in this chapter. Make a list of the types of meet ups and/or events. Identify free on inexpensive meeting space like a local coffee or tea café or library. Use an event tool like Eventbrite to manage your event planning. Promote your event with social media and on your blog and web site.

5. Here are a few more ideas—consider them extracurricular activities:

   • Visit the Digital Sisterhood Network web site to check out the initiatives. http://digitalsisterhood.wordpress.com

   • If you blog, write a post about one or more of the initiatives and ask your blog audience to share their comments.

   • If you create video or podcasts, record one about one or more of the initiatives. Invite your audience to share their comments on a video or podcast.

175

- For Facebook, Google+, and LinkedIn users, strike up a conversation with your family, friends, and colleagues by posting a status update about one or more of the initiatives. Invite them to share their thoughts.

- For Google Hangout, Skype, UStream.tv, Spreecast, and live stream users, host a live chat about one or more of the initiatives. Invite your audience to share their thoughts.

- For Flickr, Instagram, and Pinterest users, post a photo or image that reflects one or more of the initiatives. Encourage your followers to comment.

- Meet a digital sister face-to-face to chat about the discoveries you made while reading this chapter. Use Facebook or Foursquare to check in at your meet up location. Please be careful when you check in. Perhaps you can do the check in when you are leaving the location for safety precautions. Also, be mindful of how much information you share while checking in. Memorialize your meet up with a photo. Consider posting it on Facebook, Flickr, Google+, Instagram, LinkedIn, Pinterest, or Twitter after you have left the meet up location.

- Go a step further and tweet about one or more of the initiatives. Invite your Twitter friends to join the conversation. Use the hashtag #dsninitiatives. Be sure to send me a tweet about your conversation. I am @anandaleeke and @digitalsisterhd on Twitter. See you online!

Digital Sisterhood Notes Section

Feel free to use the following pages to write your responses to the chapter exercises, to journal your aha moments, to record golden nuggets of wisdom, or to take notes on whatever pops up in your gorgeous mind! Happy writing!

Ananda Kiamsha Madelyn Leeke

Digital Sisterhood Notes Section

Digital Sisterhood Notes Section

Ananda Kiamsha Madelyn Leeke

Digital Sisterhood Notes Section

© Leigh Mosley

CHAPTER FIFTEEN

EVANGELISTA EMBRACES HER HEART OF HAITI

"I found my voice when social media entered my life. I realized that a significant contribution doesn't have to look like time or money. I can actually do as much or more good by using my innate abilities to tell a story and to connect that story to those who can activate it." Ana Flores, author of Bilingual is Better *and co-founder of SpanglishBaby.com*

In 2010, I met Danica Kombol, Founding and Managing Partner of Everywhere, a social media marketing firm, during a networking session held at the Blogalicious Weekend Conference in Miami, Florida. Danica informed me about the work her firm was doing with the Heart of Haiti Campaign. Macy's, Fairwinds Trading, and the Clinton Bush Haiti Fund established the Campaign to provide sustainable income to Haitian artisans impacted by the 2010 earthquake. Our conversation naturally shifted to the role Erzulie, the Haitian goddess of love, healing, and femininity, plays in my artwork and novel, *Love's Troubadours*.

Soon after, she introduced me to Willa Shalit, CEO of Fairwinds Trading and Haitian artists Pascale Faubas and Serge Jolimeau. Willa's commitment, energy, and passion for working with the Haitian artisans convinced me to visit the Heart of Haiti booth to learn how I could use my social media influence to provide support. When I returned home from Blogalicious, I started serving as a Blogger Ambassador by writing blogs, posting Facebook status updates and Flickr photos, tweeting, recording Cinchcast podcasts, and hosting

Internet radio shows about the Heart of Haiti artisans and the people, culture, music, and spirituality of Haiti. Using my creative gifts and voice in social media to tell the story of Haitian artisans and connect it to those who can take action outside of Haiti came natural for me. My natural inclination to support Haiti and its artisans came from my passion and belief in the power of social media for social good.

The Road to Haiti

When I learned about Everywhere's Blogger Ambassador opportunity to travel to Haiti to meet with the Heart of Haiti artisans, I decided to apply. Here's an excerpt from the blog post I submitted:

> *My love affair with Haiti began when I enrolled in my first French class as a sophomore at St. Elizabeth Ann Seton High School in 1979. During that year, I became fascinated with French speaking countries in the African Diaspora. Haiti's historical legacy as the first Black republic quickly made it one of my personal favorites.*
>
> *My passion for Haiti and Haitian-influenced art was deepened during my college years as a French major at Morgan State University from 1982 to 1986. Through my studies I discovered the work of Dr. Lois Mailou Jones, an artist and professor of art at Howard University. Jones' Haitian-inspired work that included Vodun veves captivated my psyche and stayed there until I began my own studies of Vodun spirituality in the 1990s.*
>
> *Meeting my Haitian American college roommate and Sigma Gamma Rho Sorority sister Marie Denise (Mirabeau) Simon and her Haitian mother "Mama Freda" in 1985 helped me develop an interest in the lives of Haitian women. During one of our many conversations, Mama Freda told me about*

her early life in Haiti, how she studied nursing in Canada, and later moved to New York City to work as a nurse. Her stories were filled with moments when she reached into her spirit for courage and faith to live beyond any limitations people or society placed on her.

My interest in Haitian women blossomed into a full blown passion during the United Nations Fourth World Conference on Women held in Beijing, China in 1995. While in Beijing, I learned about the history of Ligue Feminine d'Action Sociale or Women's League for Social Action, the first Haitian feminist organization.

During the 1990s, I spent a lot of time learning about the Haitian love and healing goddess Erzulie, the Haitian god of the crossroads Papa Elegba, and Haitian Vodun symbols called veves. Since then, their energy has inspired my writing and art. In 2007, my debut novel Love's Troubadours—Karma: Book One was published and included artwork on the cover and inside of the book that was inspired by Erzulie's veve. Erzulie is also a dynamic force in the life of Love's Troubadours' main character. Papa Elegba makes his grand appearance in poetry and reflections included in my most recent book That Which Awakens Me: A Creative Woman's Poetic Memoir of Self-Discovery.

Writing the blog post was transformative. It solidified my identity as an Evangelista, a woman who supports and advocates a philosophy, a values system, a lifestyle, a cause, or a campaign that improves her life and others' lives. Within a few months, I received an email with news I had been selected by the Clinton Bush Fund to travel to Haiti.

Traveling to Haiti

My fellow Heart of Haiti "tripsters" included:

- Laura Ciocia, Senior Digital Strategist at Everywhere,
- Sloane Berrent Davidson, Humanitarian, Kiva Fellow, and Founder of The Causemopolitan blog,
- Deana Jirak, Designer and Photographer,
- Danica Kombol, Managing and Founding Partner at Everywhere,
- Johnica Reed, Travel Tastemaker and Writer, and
- Heather Whaling, PR/Social Media Expert and President of Geben Communication.

I learned so much about these ladies during our trip. We talked about many issues as we toured Port-au-Prince. Stories, insights, reflections, and lessons learned danced in and out of our daily adventures. Laughter, silent pauses, a reflection and prayer circle, yoga before sunrise, Reiki healing touch sessions, blogging and tweeting in the hotel restaurant, filming video interviews, taking photos everyplace we stopped, and late night girl weekend conversations are just a few of the ways we connected. In that short time, we became The Heart of Haiti Digital Sisterhood. The best phrase to describe it is in Kreyol: *belle bagay* (fabulous)!

Experiencing Haiti

My second day in Haiti began with a visit to the Presidential Palace in Port-au-Prince. As the van pulled up in front of the Presidential Palace, I heard the sound of a marching band. Men dressed in matching band uniforms played beautiful music as I surveyed the earthquake damage. I looked across the street and saw the tent camps in Champ de Mars plaza and wondered how music could be made in the midst of heartbreaking devastation. As I watched Haitian people moving through their morning with grace and dignity, the answer came in the form of a six-word memoir: Faith + Hope + Determination + Resiliency + Creativity = HAITI.

The next stop was Croix-des-Bouquets, a town located outside of Port-au-Prince, bubbling with the creativity of artisans. There I met the talented Heart of Haiti metal artisans, learned about their work and how it is made from recycled oil cans, and purchased several pieces as gifts for family and friends. Their work reminded me of Ogoun, the Haitian Vodun warrior spirit who presides over metal work, fire, hunting, politics, war, and the unemployed. Ogoun gives strength through prophecy and magic, and is known as the Father of technology and one of the husbands of Erzulie. I felt the presence of Ogoun in Jolimeau's atelier and recorded a video about it for my YouTube channel.

Right before our group ate lunch, we traveled to College Marie Reine Immaculee, a convent operated by a soulful order of nuns called Les Filles de Reine Marie Immaculee d'Haiti. The nuns help to run a national initiative for PeaceQuilts that teaches Haitian women quilting skills and incorporates Haiti's long tradition of fine needlework into each quilt. I was able to meet the women quilters and take pictures of their work. The nuns prepared a delicious lunch and gave us a sweet prayer song as a parting gift.

The final stop of the day was a visit to Komisyon Fanm Viktim pou Viktim (KOFAVIV—Commission of Women Victims for Victims), a Haitian women's organization established by and for women and girls who experience rape and other forms of violence. We had a very eye-opening and intense meeting with KOFAVIV staff and young women who were living in the tent camps. The young women shared their stories of rape, violence, and survival. They also discussed how KOFAVIV was helping them to transform their lives with counseling, computer training, and microenterprise efforts.

During our group tour of KOFAVIV's facilities, I spoke with a young woman about her life and answered questions about mine. She asked me for my email so we could stay in touch. We also took several photos together. When I returned home, I sent her an email with the photos and told her how proud she looked as she displayed her hand-painted picture frames.

My KOFAVIV support continued when I learned that Fairwinds Trading had worked with the young women to create beaded necklaces that included heart-shaped pendants created by the metal artisans and sold them to Anthropologie, a company that sells women's clothing, accessories, and home decor. I purchased several necklaces as giveaway items for my weekly #DigitalSisterhood Wednesday celebration on Twitter.

A month after I returned from Haiti, I hosted an episode of Digital Sisterhood Radio that featured a juicy discussion about the digital sisterhood experiences my fellow Heart of Haiti "tripsters" and I experienced. It gave each of us an opportunity to reflect on our most powerful moments and the relationships we developed with Fairwinds Trading staff in Haiti: Pascale Faubas, Jacmel Director, and Nathalie Tancrede, Haiti Country Director. I spoke about how the experience solidified my lifetime love affair with Haiti and her artisans, and commitment to help Haitian women. In that moment, I knew I had become an Evangelista, a woman who supports and advocates a philosophy, a values system, a lifestyle, a cause, or a campaign that improves her life and others' lives.

Writing Exercises: Your Heart

Get a pen and a piece of paper, or turn on your smartphone, iPad, tablet, netbook, laptop, or desktop computer, and reflect on what touches your heart by answering the questions below.

1. Has your heart ever been touched by an online campaign or cause?
2. How did you respond?
3. What online campaigns or causes would you like to support?
4. Here are a few more ideas—consider them extracurricular activities:

    • If you blog, write a post about one or more of your responses above and ask your blog audience to share their comments.

    • If you create video or podcasts, record one about one or more of your responses above. Invite your audience to share their comments on a video or podcast.

    • For Facebook, Google+, and LinkedIn users, strike up a conversation with your family, friends, and colleagues by posting a status update about one or more of your responses above. Invite them to share their thoughts.

    • For Google Hangout, Skype, UStream.tv, Spreecast, and live stream users, host a live chat about one or more of your responses above. Invite your audience to share their thoughts.

    • For Flickr, Instagram, and Pinterest users, post a photo or image that illustrates one or more of your responses above. Encourage your followers to comment.

    • Meet a digital sister face-to-face to chat about the discoveries you made while reading this chapter. Use Facebook or Foursquare to check in at your meet up location. Please be careful when you check in. Perhaps you can do the check in when you are leaving the location for safety precautions. Also, be mindful of how much information you share while checking in. Memorialize your meet up with a photo. Consider posting it on Facebook, Flickr, Google+, Instagram, LinkedIn, Pinterest, or Twitter after you have left the meet up location.

• Go a step further and tweet about one or more of your responses above. Invite your Twitter friends to join the conversation. Use the hashtag #dsheartcampaign. Be sure to send me a tweet about your conversation. I am @anandaleeke and @digitalsisterhd on Twitter. See you online!

Digital Sisterhood Notes Section

Feel free to use the following pages to write your responses to the chapter exercises, to journal your aha moments, to record golden nuggets of wisdom, or to take notes on whatever pops up in your gorgeous mind! Happy writing!

Ananda Kiamsha Madelyn Leeke

Digital Sisterhood Notes Section

Digital Sisterhood Notes Section

Digital Sisterhood Notes Section

CHAPTER SIXTEEN

SPELMAN COLLEGE:
A DIGITAL DOYENNE TRAILBLAZER

"Academic excellence and leadership development are hallmarks of the Spelman education, which includes preparing young women to excel in the areas of technology and digital media. Technology plays a major role in our lives. Success in this area is pivotal to our success as a city and as a country to remain globally competitive." Dr. Beverly Daniel Tatum, President of Spelman College

Strolling across Spelman College's campus for the first time in 2008, I felt like I was planting the seeds of a special relationship. I was there to visit landmarks I wrote about in my novel, *Love's Troubadours* such as the Spelman Museum of Fine Arts, a place I only knew through articles, books, and YouTube videos. Since then, I have served as speaker for Spelman's Digital Moving Image Salon's Digital Doyennes: Wisdom from Women Who Lead in Social Media and Digital Innovation event and the Eighth Annual Women of Color Leadership Conference. I attended Women Interactive, a Creative Technology Festival for women of color who produce and share digital content. I have also tracked the unique ways Spelman uses social media and technology to promote its mission, academic programs, research, students, professors, alumni, social justice efforts, and community activities.

In 2010, I watched Spelman break new media ground by co-sponsoring *Vision to Visionaries: Women Empowered*, a Legacy of Change event and live video webcast with the National Visionary Leadership Project that featured Ruby Dee, Dr. Johnetta B. Cole, Dr. Camille O. Cosby, Jasmin Guy, Jackie Joyner-Kersee, Morgan Pierce, Dr. Sonia Sanchez, and Spelman President Dr. Beverly Daniel Tatum. Spelman students including Lauren Brown Jarvis, Spelman's first social media coordinator, live tweeted the event. Later that year, I interviewed Jarvis about her academic journey and social media experiences on Digital Sisterhood Radio. Our interview helped me develop a working relationship with Spelman's Office of Communications and Digital Moving Image Salon that allowed me to provide media support through Digital Sisterhood Network's blog, social media platforms, and Talkshoe.com radio show. That's how I became familiar with the wide array of social media tools Spelman uses including Twitter, Facebook, YouTube, Flickr, blogs, ezines, and webcasts.

Guess what social media tool is a big hit at Spelman? Twitter. The college maintains the following Twitter accounts that support several departments, events, and programs:

- Spelman College—Official,
- Spelman Admissions,
- Cooperative Education,
- Dual Degree Program,
- Scholarships,
- Human Resources,
- Senior Legacy,
- Spelman's Independent Scholars Oral History,
- Spelman Bonner Program and Community Service,
- Spelman Bookstore,
- Spelman College Media,
- Spelman College Museum of Fine Art,
- Spelman Public Safety,
- Spelman Wellness, and
- Women of Color Conference.

Dr. Tatum is a top-notch Twitter Ambassador. Her Twitterstream is decorated with a collection of moments from her daily life and travel adventures, shout outs to students and staff, news about campus activities and alumni, reflections and soundbytes from conferences and meetings, words of wisdom, inspiring quotes, event photos and videos, and donor requests. Through her tweets, students, parents, faculty, alumni, donors, community organizations, corporate partners, and the general public, get a snapshot of what it means to lead Spelman women in the 21st century.

Through Dr. Tatum's leadership, the Division of Student Affairs has ensured that Spelman women use social media effectively and wisely by providing a guide and related materials on social media decorum. Students are required to read and sign the Standards of Excellence Honor Code which includes a section on social networking. They are also offered student leadership training sessions to raise social media awareness. These efforts mirror Spelman's social media policies.

Spelman students harnessed their social media power in a video campaign to land First Lady Michelle Obama as their 2011 commencement speaker. Their efforts were successful. On May 15, 2011, Mrs. Obama delivered a powerful address that is available now on Spelman's YouTube Channel. I have to admit I watch it regularly for inspiration. My favorite part of the video is towards the end when Mrs. Obama quotes the words of author Tina McElroy Ansa, Spelman class of 1971: "Claim what is yours . . . You belong anywhere on this earth you want to." I think these words describe the approach Spelman takes in expanding its presence in the digital world. That's why StudentAdvisor.com named Spelman as one of the Top 100 Social Media Colleges (ranked 21st) in 2011.

Spelman students are also expanding their presence in the digital world through the Robotics Club a/k/a The SpelBots, an all-female robotics team that encourages students to explore robotics and computer science. In 2011, *Inside Spelman* reported that the Spelbots received a $525,000 grant from the National Science Foundation to fund and expand STEM outreach. SpelBots also created a mobile application. In 2010, AT&T announced Spelmanites Jonecia Keels and Jazmine Miller won the 2010 AT&T Big Mobile on Campus Challenge with their HBCU Buddy, an iPhone application created to educate and inform users about historically Black colleges and universities in the United States. Keels and Miller received $5,000 each, a mobile device of their choice, a lifetime development license for Spelman, and all-expense paid trips to the AT&T Higher Ed Board of Advisors meeting and the EDUCAUSE Annual Conference.

I could go on and on about Spelman, but I will end this chapter by saying three things:

- Spelman women embody digital sisterhood.
- I am a Spelman fan for life!
- You can become one too when you LIKE them on Facebook, follow them on Twitter @SpelmanCollege, and support them financially by making a donation. Visit www.spelman.edu.

Written Exercises: Your Digital Doyennes

Doyenne is a French word that refers to a woman who is the most experienced and respected member or leader of a group or profession of a business, community, institution, organization, or profession. It could also refer to a woman-led business, institution, or organization. Get a pen and a piece of paper, or turn on your smartphone, iPad, tablet, netbook, laptop, or desktop computer, and reflect on the digital doyenne trailblazers in your life by answering the questions below.

1. Cheryl Mayberry McKissack is Chief Operating Officer of Johnson Publishing Company. McKissack is also the founder, President, and CEO of Nia Enterprises, LLC, a Chicago-based research and marketing services firm. In 2000, she launched NiaOnline.com, one of the first online communities created by and for African American women. I met and interviewed her during the Blogalicious Weekend Conference in 2009. At the end of her video interview, she challenged me to commit to building and maintaining collaborative relationships with other women of color in the digital space. In that moment, I realized she was an Internet institution builder who leads, encourages, and mentors wherever she goes. She became a digital doyenne in my life. Who are the digital doyennes in your life that build Internet institutions?
2. What lessons have you learned from your digital doyennes?
3. Here are a few more ideas—consider them extracurricular activities:

    *   If you blog, write a post about one or more of your responses above and ask your blog audience to share their comments.

    *   If you create video, audio blogs, or podcasts, record one about one or more of your responses above. Invite your audience to share their comments on a video, audio blog, or podcast.

- For Facebook, Google+, and LinkedIn users, strike up a conversation with your family, friends, and colleagues by posting a status update about one or more of your responses above. Invite them to share their thoughts.

- For Google Hangout, Skype, UStream.tv, Spreecast, and live stream users, host a live chat about one or more of your responses above. Invite your audience to share their thoughts.

- For Flickr, Instagram, and Pinterest users, post a photo or image that illustrates one or more of your responses above. Encourage your followers to comment.

- Meet a digital sister face-to-face to chat about the discoveries you made while reading this chapter. Use Facebook or Foursquare to check in at your meet up location. Please be careful when you check in. Perhaps you can do the check in when you are leaving the location for safety precautions. Also, be mindful of how much information you share while checking in. Memorialize your meet up with a photo. Consider posting it on Facebook, Flickr, Google+, Instagram, LinkedIn, Pinterest, or Twitter after you have left the meet up location.

- Go a step further and tweet about one or more of your responses above. Invite your Twitter friends to join the conversation. Use the hashtag #dsdoyenne. Be sure to send me a tweet about your conversation. I am @anandaleeke and @digitalsisterhd on Twitter. See you online!

Digital Sisterhood Notes Section

Feel free to use the following pages to write your responses to the chapter exercises, to journal your aha moments, to record golden nuggets of wisdom, or to take notes on whatever pops up in your gorgeous mind! Happy writing!

Digital Sisterhood Notes Section

Digital Sisterhood Notes Section

Ananda Kiamsha Madelyn Leeke

Digital Sisterhood Notes Section

PART FOUR

FIERCE LIVING 4.0

"In the long run, we shape our lives, and we shape ourselves. The process never ends until we die. And the choices we make are ultimately our own responsibility." Eleanor Roosevelt, *United Nations Diplomat, Humanitarian, and First Lady*

"When you define your life as a work of art, each brush stroke, each decision, each piece has significant value." Kimberly Wilson, *author of* Hip Tranquil Chick: A Guide to Life On and Off the Yoga Mat *and* Tranquilista: Mastering the Art of Enlightened Work and Mindful Play, *eco-fashion designer, entrepreneur, and yoga teacher*

© Leigh Mosley

CHAPTER SEVENTEEN

Flowista Unplugs and Chooses Fierce Living

"Unplugging completely allows us some time to reflect on the ways in which we want to engage. It allows us to reengage mindfully, purposefully." Gwen Bell, author of Digital Warriorship

On the first day of 2012, I wrote in my journal:

2012 must be different from 2011. I must return to the deep, juicy space of creativity that I discovered in 1992, the year I baptized myself in poetry, meditation, journal writing, self-publishing my own work, art, daydreaming, museum and gallery visits, and travel adventures. I must come home to myself.

I must let go of my need to overgive to others at my own expense. I must step back from certain relationships, let go of some that no longer serve me, and establish healthy boundaries in the ones I choose to nurture.

I must become a Flowista, a woman who unplugs from her digital life and tech toys for periods of time so she can recharge and take care of her own needs.

What road must I take?

When I start walking along the road, how do I come home to myself?

Through fierce living from your creative heart.

What's that?

Fierce Living is

F—Finding your
I—Inner women inside of you by
E—Exploring who they are and
R—Receiving them into your life as your
C—Community of
E—Expression and

When you tap into your inner women be sure to

L—Listen to them because they offer
I—Intuition
V—Vulnerability
I—Imagination
N—Nurturing and
G—Growth opportunities

This acronym became my personal theme for 2012 and a reminder of what I need to do to come home to myself.

Coming home to myself through unplugging and slowing down have allowed me to spend time reconnecting with my eight inner women otherwise known as archetypes or personalities. We've known each other for many years now. They include Ancestor, my wise woman; Ananda, my spirit woman and mystic; Kiamsha, my creative woman; Madelyn, my CEO woman; Cheryl, my balanced woman and peacekeeper; Puf, my girl child and Black American Princess;

Sapphire, my warrior woman and sexy vixen; and Broomhilda, my inner critic. We reconnected through mindful meditation, Reiki healing touch, yoga, journaling, collage making, writing an intention statement, playing with six-word memoirs, going on creative adventure dates and walks, reading magazines, listening to music, shopping for our favorite things, and playing dress up in my closet.

This investment of time helped me deeply listen to myself. I discovered I needed to do a better job of taking care of myself. I needed to practice self-compassion. I needed more "ME" time to just be, to rest, to daydream, to imagine, and to create. I needed to set better boundaries with my time, energy, resource sharing, and relationships. I also needed to say NO to certain people and requests so I could have space to say YES to the people and things that nourished my creative heart.

A few days after I started my coming home process, I received an email from Barbara Jones, the founder of the One2One Network who I met a few months earlier at Blogalicious, about speaking at BlissDom, an annual social media conference for women held in Nashville, Tennessee that Barbara and Alli Worthington, founder of Blissfully Domestic Publishing, established. After a few rounds of email with Megan Jordan, BlissDom's Content & Speaker Coordinator, I was confirmed as a speaker for a session on "Fierce Living from Your Creative Heart." Now that was magical for me because I was getting a chance to teach and share my new approach to living.

Bringing Fierce Living to the BlissDom 2012 Conference

The morning of my BlissDom session began with meditation, prayer, yoga, and Reiki healing touch in my lovely room at the Opryland Hotel. During my morning spiritual practice, I focused on opening my heart and surrendering to Creator's highest good. I made sure to say a prayer of thanksgiving for blessing me with an opportunity to share my gifts as a creative professional with an amazing community of women and men bloggers. Afterwards, I got dressed, packed my conference bag with my workshop materials, and headed to breakfast.

Breakfast was yummy! I ate plenty of delicious fruit and two chocolate muffins as I watched the powerful opening video and listened to the "Bliss Chicks" Alli, Barbara, and Paula Bruno welcome everyone to BlissDom. The morning got better as I sat writing notes during author and blogger Jon Acuff's keynote address. It ended with entrepreneurial inspiration from Alli and Latinos in Social Media founder Ana Roca Castro's introduction of Picha Global, a social media business they formed with Barbara and Megan.

The positive BlissDom breakfast energy followed me into Jeannette Kaplun's session, "Living (and Embracing) the Best of the Life You Have Created for Yourself." Jeannette reminded me to choose joy, grace, gratitude, ease, acceptance, forgiveness, and peace in my daily life. The morning events filled my heart with so much joy and positive energy, and affirmed that BlissDom was indeed the perfect place for me to share my insights on how I discovered fierce living from my creative heart.

Before I began my session, I took a minute to take in the faces of the BlissDom attendees. I smiled inside and outside because we were about to learn and grow together. My session began with the following introduction.

> *Welcome to "Fierce Living from Your Creative Heart." Fierce Living is a journey worth taking in 2012. It begins with an open heart in the present moment. When you breathe intentionally and deeply, you invite yourself into the present moment. You also create space to discover who you are from the inside out and what's happening in your creative heart. So let's get started.*

The yoga teacher inside of me always makes sure breathing exercises are included in my workshop sessions. Here are the ones I shared that day.

> *Join me in taking 10 deep breaths. We inhale through our noses and exhale through our mouths. Feel free to make sounds like hah as you exhale. You can get loud too.*

- *Take a deep breath and inhale self-love. Exhale anything that gets in the way of you experiencing it.*
- *Inhale self-care. Exhale anything that gets in the way of you experiencing it.*
- *Inhale self-expression. Exhale anything that gets in the way of you experiencing it.*
- *Inhale self-discovery. Exhale anything that gets in the way of you experiencing it.*
- *Inhale vulnerability. Exhale anything that gets in the way of you tapping into it.*
- *Inhale intuition. Exhale anything that gets in the way of you tapping into it.*
- *Inhale imagination. Exhale anything that gets in the way of you tapping into it.*
- *Inhale inspiration. Exhale anything that gets in the way of you tapping into it.*
- *Inhale creativity. Exhale anything that gets in the way of you tapping into it.*
- *Inhale gratitude. Exhale anything that gets in the way of you expressing it.*

> *In this sacred place, quietly set an intention for your session today. An intention is a statement about what you want to experience. When you are done, open your eyes.*

The next exercise focused on one of my favorites: six-word memoirs. I asked the group to write a present moment six-word memoir which is composed of six words that expressed how they were feeling in the present moment. During the group sharing circle, I listened to the authentic, beautiful, creative, and vulnerable statements people wrote. It was powerful to witness.

After the six-word memoir writing exercise, I gave a five-minute talk that discussed my 2012 wake-up call and realization of fierce living from my creative heart. The session continued with more breathing and writing exercises that invited each attendee to explore what their creative heart looked and felt like, what their creative heart needs and wants in 2012, who their inner women are and what they want them to know, and their definition of fierce living. The group engaged in deep discussion after each exercise. Aha moments, tears, sighs, laughter, joy, and a range of emotions and thoughts were shared. At the end of the session, my creative heart was filled with humility and gratitude for each person in the room. The experience reaffirmed my calling to do creative coaching and write and publish my books.

Fierce Living Commitments

When I returned home from BlissDom, I made six "fierce living" commitments based on what I learned during the conference.

- To embrace my visual voice with digital photographs and videos that record authentic moments and tell stories.
- To affirm my visual voice by sharing what I create on my blog, Animoto, Facebook, Flickr, Google+, Instagram, Pinterest, Twitter, Tumblr, and YouTube.
- To nurture my creative spirit weekly with journaling, artist dates, and reading time (articles, blogs, books, and online creative communities).
- To affirm, fully claim, and respect my creative journey as an artist in a professional manner.
- To seek and pursue ways to expand my professional career as an artist.
- To respect and treat my creativity as a business.

Here's the good news! I was able to take action on all of my new commitments the following month. For instance, I started carrying my digital camera with me every day. That helped me capture my favorite springtime moments. I was able to share my digital photos on my blog, Facebook, Flickr, Google+, Instagram, Pinterest, Twitter, and Tumblr. It felt great to receive positive feedback from my social media friends. I created three videos with Animoto that featured my photos from BlissDom and artwork. The videos were posted on my blog, Facebook, Google+, Twitter, Tumblr, and YouTube. Posting the videos gave me much needed feedback and helped me see the value in sharing my work with others.

In addition, I started reading Kelly Rae Roberts' book, *Taking Flight: Inspiration and Techniques To Give Your Creative Spirit Wings*. The book's journaling exercises helped me get in touch with my creative spirit. I also took a walking tour of galleries in my neighborhood: Joan Hisaoka Healing Arts Gallery, Morton Fine Art Gallery, and Hamiltonian Gallery. Seeing new art created by a diverse group of artists was inspiring.

And here's the HUGE leap I took to expand my professional career as an artist: submitting my application to the Hamiltonian Fellowship Program. The application process required me to write an artist statement and artist curriculum vitae (CV), and prepare a digital portfolio of ten pieces of artwork. After I finished my application, I decided to post my artist statement and CV on my web site. Although my application was not accepted, the process helped me affirm my professional career as an artist and respect and treat my creativity as a business.

Written Exercises: Your Fierce Living

Get a pen and a piece of paper, or turn on your smartphone, iPad, tablet, netbook, laptop, or desktop computer, and reflect on fierce living in your life by answering the questions below.

1. What does fierce living mean to you?
2. How have you expressed fierce living in your life?
3. Embracing "fierce living" practices helped me unplug from my digital life and become a Flowista on many occasions. As a Flowista, I have learned the value of what Sherry Turkle, author of *Alone Together: Why We Expect More From Technology and Less From Each Other*, writes about: "what technology makes easy is not always what nurtures the human spirit." Taking a break from technology helps me take better care of my spirit, heart, mind, and body. It allows me to be more present to myself and others. Have you unplugged from your digital life? How do you feel when you unplug? How does it impact the way you care for your spirit, heart, mind, and body? How does it affect your interactions and relationships with others?
4. Are you a Flowista? If not, do you want to become one? What steps do you need to take to embrace your inner Flowista?
5. 2012 was filled with many "fierce living" learning opportunities that occurred during my participation in events sponsored by BlissDom, Blogalicious, BlogHer, DigitalUnDivided, and Spelman College. After each event, I blogged and wrote in my journal about my experiences. Recently, I prepared a list of 10 takeaways that summarize the wisdom I received.

   - Discover yourself.
   - Tell your story.
   - Build a team.
   - Act like you have a team.
   - Take care of yourself.
   - Educate yourself and expand your skill set.

- Find opportunities to express your gifts and talents.
- Create, fund, price, market, and sell your products and services.
- Give back.
- Celebrate yourself and all you have done.

Have you experienced any "fierce living" learning opportunities?

6. What are your key "fierce living" takeaways from this year?
7. Have you made any "fierce living" commitments?
8. Here are a few more ideas—consider them extracurricular activities:

    - If you blog, write a post about one or more of your responses above and ask your blog audience to share their comments.

    - If you create video, audio blogs, or podcasts, record one about one or more of your responses above. Invite your audience to share their comments on a video, audio blog, or podcast.

    - For Facebook, Google+, and LinkedIn users, strike up a conversation with your family, friends, and colleagues by posting a status update about one or more of your responses above. Invite them to share their thoughts.

    - For Google Hangout, Skype, UStream.tv, Spreecast, and live stream users, host a live chat about one or more of your responses above. Invite your audience to share their thoughts.

    - For Flickr, Instagram, and Pinterest users, post a photo or image that illustrates one or more of your responses above. Encourage your followers to comment.

    - Meet a digital sister face-to-face to chat about the discoveries you made while reading this chapter. Use Facebook or

Foursquare to check in at your meet up location. Please be careful when you check in. Perhaps you can do the check in when you are leaving the location for safety precautions. Also, be mindful of how much information you share while checking in. Memorialize your meet up with a photo. Consider posting it on Facebook, Flickr, Google+, Instagram, LinkedIn, Pinterest, or Twitter after you have left the meet up location.

• Go a step further and tweet about one or more of your responses above. Invite your Twitter friends to join the conversation. Use the hashtag #fierceliving. Be sure to send me a tweet about your conversation. I am @anandaleeke and @digitalsisterhd on Twitter. See you online!

Digital Sisterhood Notes Section

Feel free to use the following pages to write your responses to the chapter exercises, to journal your aha moments, to record golden nuggets of wisdom, or to take notes on whatever pops up in your gorgeous mind! Happy writing!

Ananda Kiamsha Madelyn Leeke

Digital Sisterhood Notes Section

Digital Sisterhood Notes Section

Digital Sisterhood Notes Section

I AM
A
LIFESTYLISTA
DIGITAL SISTER!
#dslifestylista

© *Leigh Mosley*

CHAPTER EIGHTEEN

LIFESTYLISTA LOVES HERSELF AND GIVES BACK

"Self-love is a way of living, a practice, and an awareness that you carry with you as a compass and a decision guide to how to live your life." Christine Arylo, author of Madly in Love with Me: The Daring Adventure of Becoming Your Own Best Friend

It's December 1, 2012, the first day of Digital Sisterhood Month. I spent the afternoon at the TEDxAdamsMorganWomen event organized by Kety Esquivel, a digital executive at Fenton, and Suzanne Turner, founder of Turner Strategies and Feminism 2.0. The event theme was "The Space Between." A group of women and men shared their stories and insights. I also watched a part of the TEDxWomen conference hosted by Pat Mitchell and the Paley Center for Media that was livestreamed during the event. It included a talk given by Lourds Lane, a Filipino-American violinist, musical prodigy, and front woman of the band LOURDS. Lane spoke about the power of embracing and owning your full self—including your failures, fears, and flaws. Her mantra, "if you can't fix it, feature it" hit home because it reminded me that through the practice of self-love I can reach the space between my authentic self and my failures, fears, and flaws, and choose to live my best life.

Give Back to Yourself

When my self-love journey started in 1992, I used audio recordings, books, classes, conferences, creative expression, fitness, integrative medicine, meditation, music, nature, spiritual communities, therapy, vegetarianism, and yoga to support myself. The Internet expanded my access to self-love resources. One of my first online resources was the information media mogul Oprah Winfrey included on her web site after she launched her "Change Your Life TV" series. That information and the community conversations I discovered via Oprah.com's message boards inspired my self-love life practices. Today, they include:

- Nurturing and surrendering my spirit through affirmations, devotional reading, journal writing, mantra chanting, meditation, prayer, retreat and worship within a sacred community, Reiki healing touch, and yoga.
- Listening and tending to my heart through quiet time and reflection.
- Honoring my body through acupuncture, healthy eating, massage, running, walking, and weight training.
- Being curious, grateful, and open to life.
- Identifying and pursuing my passions.
- Celebrating and expressing my creativity.
- Eating, playing, and shopping in my own backyard (my neighborhood and city).
- Supporting local small businesses in my community.
- Traveling as a global citizen of the world.
- Learning continuously.
- Treating my home as a sanctuary.
- Practicing financial responsibility so that I am able to care for myself.

These practices encouraged me to read blogs like Brene Brown's OrdinaryCourage.com and Mindy Tsonas' WishStudio. com; to visit Madsyn Taylor's DailyOm.com and Takeyah Young's

CoreConnectionLifestyle.com; to follow Global Love Project founder
Aine Belton and Positively Present founder Dani DiPirro on Twitter;
to watch videos featuring the teachings of Reverend Dr. Iyanla
Vanzant; and to participate in online communities such as Lissa
Rankin's Owning Pink. These women taught me how other women
were caring for and loving themselves. They also reminded me to
invest in myself and the things that make my heart sing. As a result,
I embraced my inner Lifestylista, a woman who lives her life as a
work of art; expresses it through her passion for beauty, entertaining,
fashion, food, home décor, personal style, and travel; and inspires
others to live their lives as works of art. In addition, I was inspired to
re-launch my Tumblr blog as Ananda@16thandU: Lifestylista in Love
with DC. This blog allows me to share stories about how I integrate
my self-love practices into my lifestyle activities.

Give Back to Women Online

When I give back to myself, I have more to give back to others.
One of my favorite give back reminders is from Tara Hunt, author of
The Whuffie Factor: "figure out how you are going to give back to the
community and do it . . . often." Hunt's words connect me to what I
learned while growing up Catholic: giving back to others is a spiritual
practice that opens one's heart to the beauty of humanity. They also
helped me tap into the community service work ethic I adopted when
I became a member of Sigma Gamma Rho Sorority, Inc. and pledged
to live up to its motto, "Great Service, Greater Progress."

As I have traveled the Internet, Hunt's words and my Catholic
and sorority experiences, keep inspiring me to use my digital
influence to support campaigns and creative efforts launched
by women online that provide awareness, financial capital, and
information to improve people's lives. Here are several examples.

- Blogging for President Barack Obama's 2012 Election Campaign

During the 2012 U.S. presidential campaign, I used my author blog, Facebook, Flickr, Instagram, and Twitter to promote President Obama's re-election efforts. BarackObama.com helped me identify volunteer opportunities to do canvassing in my neighborhood and work with my dad at the phone bank located at the Obama campaign office in Prince George's County, Maryland. Contributing financially to the campaign via BarackObama.com helped me own a piece of the Obama 2012 campaign. Through MeetUp.com, I organized monthly Yoga for Obama fundraiser classes in Malcolm X-Meridian Hill Park. Seeing President Obama's live web cast at the BlogHer 2012 conference and blogging and tweeting about it was energizing. Joining the #BlogforObama community of women bloggers and live tweeting during the debates allowed me to add my support to the voices of women online. Throughout this process, I learned what Morra Aarons-Mele, CEO of Women Online, wrote about in a Huffington Post article: *"Turns out, we can use our social media networks to influence friends and followers to vote."*

- CashMob

Cash mobs are grassroots efforts that are organized as a group event to encourage people to support businesses in their local communities by showing up and purchasing products and/service at a predetermined time. They are fueled by social media. I organized a local "cash mob" during Digital Sisterhood Month 2012 to support local boutiques and vintage stores owned by people of color and women in my U Street neighborhood in D.C. For more information, visit CashMob.com.

- Crowdfunding

  Crowdfunding allows people to use the Internet to network and pool their resources to raise money that supports the development of businesses, campaigns, causes, products, and services. I learned the value and success of crowdfunding when I successfully completed two Kickstarter fundraisers for this book's publishing expenses in 2010 and 2011. As a result, I made a personal commitment to support several women's crowdfunding campaigns including:

  ➢ Kimberly Bryant's Indiegogo fundraiser for Black Girls CODE—Summer of CODE 2013—The Remix.
  ➢ Kathryn Buford's Live Unchained Indiegogo fundraiser for Terrifying, Beautiful, and Strange, an awards ceremony for women artists.
  ➢ Dariana and Dariela Cruz's Indiegogo fundraiser to help their business, Dari Design Studio prepare for and attend SUREX, the global marketplace for original art and design where artists, agents, and licensors connect with manufacturers and retailers to create products.
  ➢ Cynthia Fikes' GoFundMe.com fundraiser for her daughter Taylor Fikes' tuition to attend the Bolshoi Ballet Academy in Moscow, Russia.
  ➢ Kiratiana Freelon's Kickstarter fundraiser for the publication of *The Travel Guide to Multicultural London.*
  ➢ Shantrelle Lewis' Kickstarter fundraiser for her *Black Pete: Zwarte Piet* documentary film.
  ➢ Numa Perrier's Indiegogo fundraiser for Black & Sexy TV Collection Plate.
  ➢ Jessica Solomon's The Saartjie Project's Kickstarter fundraiser for its *Four Women* performance and GoFundMe.com fundraiser for her participation in the Urban Bush Women Summer Leadership Institute.

➤ Techturized's Indiegogo fundraiser for MadameYou.com created by Joy Buolamwini, Chanel Martin, Candace Mitchell, and Jess Watson.

➤ Dr. Marta Moreno Vega's Kickstarter fundraiser for her *Let the Spirit Move You* documentary film.

➤ Monda Webb's Kickstarter.com fundraiser for her *7:33 am the Movie* project.

➤ Jeshawna Wholley's GoFundMe.com fundraiser for her Afro-Brazilian study abroad program in Brazil.

➤ Wild Women Theatre Indiegogo fundraiser for the 2013 Capital Fringe Festival created by Jade Andwele, Margaux Delotte-Bennett, Shonda Goward, Farah Harris, and Clarissa McKithen.

➤ Takeyah Young's ChipIn.com fundraiser for a trip to work with the Edeyo Foundation and Rhythm 'N Dance on health and nutrition programming and a cultural arts education program at the Joyous Heart School in Port-Au-Prince, Haiti.

• Health Awareness Campaigns

I have utilized my author blog, Facebook page, and #DigitalSisterhood Wednesdays on Twitter to raise awareness about breast cancer, domestic violence, heart health, HIV/AIDS, mental health, sexual assault violence, and women's health issues.

• Radio Interviews

I have used my BlogTalkRadio and Talkshoe.com shows to interview women in social media and tech. The interviews highlighted their accomplishments and promoted their events, products, and services.

- Running Races

  I have used the Internet and my social media platforms to promote my participation in 5K races that raise awareness about brain tumors, breast cancer, leukemia, pancreatic cancer, and women in politics.

- Sharing Information and Inspiration

  I have shared articles, encouraging comments, inspirational quotes and stories, and all types of information with people in my social networks.

- Volunteering My Skills

  I have served as an online yoga teacher and used MomTV, Stickam.com, and YouTube to teach yoga exercises that help social media users take better care of themselves. I have also used MeetUp.com to provide free yoga classes to D.C. area residents during the spring, summer, and fall months. I developed a series of free video workshops on UStream.tv that offer creativity coaching and social media 101 training. During the annual Digital Sisterhood Month celebration, I donated creativity coaching sessions and provided one-hour Skype conference calls to women in social media.

- Voluntourism

  Voluntourism allows you to travel and volunteer for a charitable cause or organization at the same time. I used the Internet to research my trip to Cuba and identified the Cuba AIDS Project as my voluntourism experience in 2004. My email network and Yahoo groups helped me raise money and solicit supplies for my Cuba trip. When I returned, I shared stories and photos with these groups.

There are many other ways to give back to women online such as participating in and promoting their events, featuring or interviewing them on your blog or social media sites, introducing them to members of your professional network, and recommending them for a professional opportunity such as a brand ambassadorship, blogger campaign, workshop facilitator position, or speaking engagement. Whatever way you choose to give back to women online, know your support will be a blessing!

Giving Back Creates Social Capital

When you give back to others, you build relationships that create social capital, "the stuff that makes relationships meaningful and resilient," writes Alison Fine and Beth Kanter in their book, *The Networked Nonprofit: Connecting with Social Media to Drive Change*. Over the past several years, I have given back and received so many blessings from women bloggers, entrepreneurs, social media influencers, and tech professionals I've connected with. They are network weavers who make things happen by sharing information, ideas, and messages that shape conversations and offer reasons to support causes, communities, and organizations. Several have become my peer mentors. Our relationships are rooted in generosity, support, and shared interests. Over time, they have generated social capital, a level of trust and reciprocity that allows us to ask each other for advice and support for brainstorming, business opportunities, collaborative partnerships, strategic planning, and so much more.

Some of my greatest sources of social capital are my relationships with women who live in the Washington, D.C. area. I met most of them through social networking sites such as Sojournal Urban Media Network, Women for Change on Groupsite.com, and Black Author Showcase, and during conferences, events, and meet ups sponsored by Blogalicious, Crisis Camp DC, DC Digital Capital Week, DC Media Makers, Fabulous Women Business Owners DC, Feminism 2.0, Latinos in Social Media, Nonprofit 2.0, She's Geeky DC, Social Justice Camp DC, Social Media Club DC, Social Media Week

DC, and Vision Quest Retreats. What makes them so special is the fact that I have many more opportunities to interact with them in person over the course of a year. We are able to meet for coffee or tea and brainstorm about projects that make a local impact, share information that helps us expand our networks, learn together at conferences and meet ups, and show up and support each other at our events. Our interactions expand and improve our businesses, causes, campaigns, creativity, digital presence, and lives. They represent a reciprocal gateway of generosity, a priceless gift to others that gives you the inspiration to continue practicing self-love with support from women online.

Writing Exercises: Your Giving Back

Get a pen and a piece of paper, or turn on your smartphone, iPad, tablet, netbook, laptop, or desktop computer, and reflect on your giving back experiences by answering the questions below.

1. How do you give back to yourself?
2. How do you feel when you give back to yourself?
3. What prevents you from giving back to yourself?
4. How can you ensure that you will give back to yourself?
5. How do you give back to women online?
6. What ways would you like to give back to women online?
7. Here are a few more ideas—consider them extracurricular activities:

   - If you blog, write a post about one or more of your responses above and ask your blog audience to share their comments.

   - If you create video or podcasts, record one about one or more of your responses above. Invite your audience to share their comments on a video or podcast.

   - For Facebook, Google+, and LinkedIn users, strike up a conversation with your family, friends, and colleagues by posting a status update about one or more of your responses above. Invite them to share their thoughts.

   - For Google Hangout, Skype, UStream.tv, Spreecast, and live stream users, host a live chat about one or more of your responses above. Invite your audience to share their thoughts.

   - For Flickr, Instagram, and Pinterest users, post a photo or image that illustrates one or more of your responses above. Encourage your followers to comment.

- Meet a digital sister face-to-face to chat about the discoveries you made while reading this chapter. Use Facebook or Foursquare to check in at your meet up location. Please be careful when you check in. Perhaps you can do the check in when you are leaving the location for safety precautions. Also, be mindful of how much information you share while checking in. Memorialize your meet up with a photo. Consider posting it on Facebook, Flickr, Google+, Instagram, LinkedIn, Pinterest, or Twitter after you have left the meet up location.

- Go a step further and tweet about one or more of your responses above. Invite your Twitter friends to join the conversation. Use the hashtag #dsgivingback. Be sure to send me a tweet about your conversation. I am @anandaleeke and @digitalsisterhd on Twitter. See you online!

Digital Sisterhood Notes Section

Feel free to use the following pages to write your responses to the chapter exercises, to journal your aha moments, to record golden nuggets of wisdom, or to take notes on whatever pops up in your gorgeous mind! Happy writing!

Digital Sisterhood Notes Section

Digital Sisterhood Notes Section

Digital Sisterhood Notes Section

APPENDICES: DEEPENING YOUR DIGITAL SISTERHOOD EXPERIENCE

APPENDIX A

The ABCs of Digital Sisterhood

Have you ever thought about creating your own guidelines that address how you will interact online? I created mine using the ABCs as a template. Check them out below. Use the Digital Sisterhood Notes Section to create your own ABCs of Digital Sisterhood.

- A—Authenticity comes from embracing who you are, including your strengths, weaknesses, successes, failures, dreams, and fears. Always be your authentic self online and offline. It's the only way to fully express who you are.

- B—Be able to ask for help. You cannot do everything by yourself. That's why you have digital sisters and digital brothers. Reach out to your network. You never know who can help you if you don't ask. Make asking a daily and weekly ritual.

- C—Collaborate with others. It allows you to build partnerships and help your digital sisters and brothers grow bigger and better. In turn, you grow bigger and better. Collaborations are a win-win for everyone involved.

- D—Digital civility is an essential ingredient to your relationship-building skills. Be mindful of how you communicate with others. You can express your opinion and/ or disagree without harming someone with verbally abusive language, threats, or cyber bullying. In short, treat people with respect.

- E—Evolve with technology. Keep learning new information and tools at your own pace.

- F—Find social causes you believe in and support them.

- G—Generosity is a great practice to incorporate. It allows you to help another person and makes you feel good about yourself. It also creates social capital, the warm and fuzzy feeling that encourages people to help and support you.

- H—Have face-to-face meetings with your digital sisters and brothers. Meeting someone in person or via Skype, Google+ Hangout, or another video chatting service deepens the connection you have with the individual.

- I—Invest in yourself by reading articles, blogs, books, and magazines that help you learn more about yourself and your interests. Invest in yourself by attending meet ups and tweet ups, conferences, trainings, webinars, workshops, and Twitter and video chats that offer learning and networking opportunities.

- J—Join a community, MeetUp.com group, or an online discussion that you wouldn't normally participate in. Shake things up and get to know a new group of people. It will expand your network and possibly give you some fresh ideas for your own digital life.

- K—Keep a positive attitude of gratitude!

- L—Listen to what people are saying about topics that interest you online. Listen to what people are saying about you online and offline. Step back and evaluate what you learn. Make the appropriate changes and move forward.

- M—Mentoring is a wonderful personal and professional development experience. Mentor other women. Allow other women to mentor you. Create your own virtual mentors by identifying women who you admire. Call them your digital diva sheroes. Watch what they do online. Read their articles, blogs, and books. Follow them on social media. Subscribe to their newsletters. Listen to their podcasts. Watch their videos. Participate in their online and offline events.

- N—Network in your local, national, and international communities.

- O—Open your heart to the diversity of expression in the digital space. We can learn so much from people who are different from us. Celebrate the Internet's multicultural beauty and brilliance!

- P—Pay attention to where your online community is located. Engage your audience where they are.

- Q—Queendom is the best word to describe your digital space. Be a Digital Queen Bee by expressing your authentic voice in all you say, create, and do online. Be compassionate, confident, gracious, grateful, humble, kind, savvy, and able to celebrate and promote yourself and others.

- R—Relationships that offer honesty, reciprocity, trust, and support in the digital space are what solidify digital sisterhood and digital brotherhood bonds.

- S—Streamline your digital footprint. Make sure your digital footprint, which is another word for your online presence (blog, social media, visual content in the form of photos and videos, and web site), represents your authentic self with clarity.

- T—Thrive and experience the thrill of whoever you choose to be and whatever you choose to do in the digital space. Have FUN!

- U—Unplug from your digital life and to-do lists on a regular basis. Schedule your digital timeouts so you can recharge, relax, and rest. Create a digital wellness plan that allows you to practice self-care on a daily, weekly, and/or monthly basis.

    Use the Digital Sisterhood Unplugged Weekend Initiative for resources: digitalsisterhood.wordpress.com.

    Also, check out Digital Royalty founder Amy Jo Martin's ReadySetPause.com for information on how to take a four-minute break each day.

- V—Voices of women matter. Speak up when you feel called to support a campaign or cause.

- W—Women have an incredible amount of power online. Our power comes from our digital footprint (blog, online business, web site, and social media), communities, and efforts. They give birth to our platform of influence and personal responsibility as social media leaders. So "lean in" as Facebook COO Sheryl Sandberg encourages us to do and own your power as a social media leader. One last thing: use your power and platform wisely.

- X—X-ray your digital life and make a list of the blogs, communities, e-newsletters, e-zines, Internet radio shows, mobile apps, podcasts, people, social media sites, videos, and web sites that energize, inform, inspire, and motivate you. Keep this list handy when you need a dose of positive energy, inspiration, and motivation. Tap these positive resources regularly.

- Y—"Yes" is a word you should use carefully. Only say "Yes" to business opportunities, campaigns, causes, conferences, events, and partnerships that resonate with your heart and deepest passion. Use the word "No" to create space for you to say "Yes" to what truly matters in your life. When you are able to create healthy boundaries around what you invest your energy and time in, you are giving yourself the gift of "Fierce Living."

- Z—Zero in on what you dream about, what you are good at, what you believe in, what you are passionate about, and what you need to manifest your dreams into reality. Then develop an outline of a plan and a team of people you can ask for support to help you create, build, and fund your dreams.

Ananda Kiamsha Madelyn Leeke

Digital Sisterhood Notes Section

Digital Sisterhood Notes Section

APPENDIX B

WHAT TYPE OF SOCIAL MEDIA LEADER ARE YOU?

This appendix includes an excerpt from the social media leadership sessions I facilitated during the BlogHer conference in 2013.

Do you have a blog with at least one blog reader? Do you use social media and have at least one fan, follower, or friend? If you answered "yes" to these questions, you have digital power and a digital platform of influence.

Your digital power consists of your digital footprint (blog, online business, web site, and social media), communities, and efforts. Your digital platform of influence is derived from the effect you have on your blog readers and social media fans, followers, and friends when you:

- Advocate for causes.
- Build communities.
- Create mobile applications, art, books, businesses, content, products, publications, services, tools, and webisodes.
- Curate content.
- Educate and inform.
- Give voice to your thoughts as subject matter experts, thought leaders, and brand ambassadors.
- Share information and experiences.

- Explore and experiment with new technologies as early adopters and trendsetters.
- Participate in social good campaigns.
- Inspire and motivate.
- Mentor.
- Network.
- Tell your personal stories.
- Promote and celebrate the expertise, gifts, and talents of others.

As you engage in these activities, your blog readers and social media fans, followers, and friends are watching what you say and do online. They are learning from your example. Whether you know it or not, you are leading them and have become a social media leader.

Based on my work with the Digital Sisterhood Leadership Project, I have identified 12 key leadership roles social media leaders play: advocate, community builder, creator, curator, educator, influencer, mentor, motivator, promoter, social do gooder, storyteller, and thought leader. I have used these roles to create the profiles of seven Digital Sisterhood Leadership Archetypes that you can use to develop your own leadership style and approach. They include Creativista, Empirista, Empowerista, Enchantista, Evangelista, Flowista, and Lifestylista.

To help you understand and identify your Leadership Archetypes, I have prepared a profile for each one. It includes a definition, manifesto, and the types of chakras (seven energy centers that coincide with your body's endocrine system), colors (associated with the chakras), gemstones (associated with the chakras), goddesses (feminine archetypes), and yoga poses (associated with the chakras) that correspond to each Leadership Archetype. This information is meant to spark your interest. If you would like more information, check out the web sites below.

o Archetypes: archetypeme.com
o Chakras, Colors, and Gemstones: chakraenergy.com
o Goddesses: goddess-guide.com
o Yoga Poses: yogajournal.com

Also, I encourage you to Google the topics and find articles, blogs, books, online communities, web sites, and videos to expand your knowledge base. Only use what you find is helpful. Now turn the page and dive into each profile. Use the Digital Sisterhood Notes Section to make notes. Enjoy!

CREATIVISTA PROFILE

Definition: A Creativista is a woman who gives birth to creativity (art, books, content, films, mobile apps, products, services, webisodes, and videos).

Manifesto: I am a woman who makes beautiful things. I embrace Virginia Woolf's wisdom: "No need to hurry. No need to sparkle. No need to be anybody but oneself." I create a life I love. It starts with a desire to chase what moves me the most. I discover it. I live it. I own it. I add my own scenery. I am colorful. I use my voice. I express myself. I take a deep breath and dream big. I rediscover myself. I am intuitive, open-minded, imaginative, adventurous, and curious. I am creative inside and out!

Chakra Connection: Creativista's energy is connected to the:

- Sacral, or second chakra, which corresponds to creativity, pleasure, sexuality, and well-being. It governs the bladder, circulatory system, and sexual and reproductive organs.
- Solar plexus, or third chakra, which corresponds to willpower, persistence, self-worth, self-confidence, and self-esteem. It governs the stomach, small intestine, liver, gallbladder, and spleen.
- Heart, or fourth chakra, which corresponds to love, joy, harmony, and inner peace. It governs the heart, chest, lungs, and circulation.
- Throat, or fifth chakra, which corresponds to communication, expressions of feelings, and the truth. It governs the throat, ears, nose, teeth, mouth, and neck.
- Third-eye, or sixth chakra, which corresponds to intuition, imagination, wisdom, and the ability to think and make decisions. It governs the eyes and base of the skull.

Color Connection: Wear or surround yourself with the colors orange (second chakra), yellow (third chakra), green or pink (fourth chakra), light or sky blue (fifth chakra), and indigo blue (sixth chakra) to connect with Creativista's energy.

Gemstone Connection: Wear or surround yourself with amber or carnelian (second chakra), citrine or tiger's eye (third chakra), aventurine or rose quartz (fourth chakra), turquoise (fifth chakra), and lapis lazuli (sixth chakra) gemstones to connect with Creativista's energy.

Goddess Connection:

- Oshun, the Yoruba goddess of creativity, and Sarasvati, the Hindu goddess of the arts (second chakra)
- Al-Uzza, the Arabian goddess of confidence, vigilance, and preparation; Amaterasu, the Japanese sun goddess of royal power; Durga, the Hindu warrior goddess; and Sekhmet, the Egyptian warrior goddess (third chakra)
- Aphrodite, the Greek goddess of love; Erzulie, the Haitian goddess of love; Kwan Yin, the Chinese goddess of compassion; and Venus, the Roman goddess of love, (fourth chakra)
- Vach, the Hindu goddess of speech and communication (fifth chakra)
- Tara, the Tibetan goddess of wisdom (sixth chakra)

Yoga Connection: Practicing bound angle, downward facing dog, triangle, and wide angle poses (second chakra); bow, boat, warrior one, warrior two, warrior three, sun salutation, and all twisting poses (third chakra); camel, cat, cobra, fish, sphinx, upward facing dog, and upward facing bow poses (fourth chakra); bridge, fish, lion, plow, and upward plank poses (fifth chakra); and bridge, child's, downward facing dog, shoulder stand, and standing half forward bend poses (sixth chakra) can help you connect with Creativista's energy.

EMPIRISTA PROFILE

Definition: An Empirista is a woman who thinks of herself as CEO of her own corporation, ME, Inc.; maintains an entrepreneurial mindset; and gives birth to ideas and transforms them into businesses, economies, institutions, networks, and organizations that add value to people's lives.

Manifesto: I am a woman whose time has come as an entrepreneur, trailblazer, thought leader and pioneer. I am amazing in motion, taking aim, and leading by example. *Carpe Diem* is my mantra. It helps me start something that matters. It reminds me I got the power. So I own it. I can do what I love and love the rewards. All I have to do is focus, dream it, plan it, and do it. I can take it to the next level when I think outside of the box, act boldly, spark a change, and have fun. Being confident and taking risks makes me unstoppable. I build, adapt, develop diverse perspectives, plot the future, and even make mistakes. I own my tomorrow now!

Chakra Connection: Empirista's energy is connected to the:

- Root, or first, chakra which corresponds to survival issues including food, shelter, money, and financial independence. It governs the feet, legs, bones, and spine.
- Sacral, or second chakra, which corresponds to creativity, pleasure, sexuality, and well-being. It governs the bladder, circulatory system, and sexual and reproductive organs.
- Solar plexus, or third chakra, which corresponds to willpower, persistence, self-worth, self-confidence, and self-esteem. It governs the stomach, small intestine, liver, gallbladder, and spleen.
- Third-eye, or sixth chakra, which corresponds to intuition, imagination, wisdom, and the ability to think and make decisions. It governs the eyes and base of the skull.

Color Connection: Wear or surround yourself with the colors red (first chakra), orange (second chakra), yellow (third chakra), and indigo blue (sixth chakra) to connect with Empirista's energy.

Gemstone Connection: Wear or surround yourself with garnet or ruby (first chakra), amber or carnelian (second chakra), citrine or tiger's eye (third chakra), and lapis lazuli (sixth chakra) gemstones to connect with Empirista's energy.

Goddess Connection:

- Atira, the Pawnee Native American goddess of the earth; Coatlicue, the Mexican goddess of the earth; and Gaia, the Greek goddess of the earth (first chakra)
- Oshun, the Yoruba goddess of creativity, and Sarasvati, the Hindu goddess of the arts (second chakra)
- Al-Uzza, the Arabian goddess of confidence, vigilance, and preparation; Amaterasu, the Japanese sun goddess of royal power; Durga, the Hindu warrior goddess; and Sekhmet, the Egyptian warrior goddess (third chakra)
- Tara, the Tibetan goddess of wisdom (sixth chakra)

Yoga Connection: Practicing mountain, warrior two, standing forward fold, and bridge poses (first chakra); bound angle, downward facing dog, triangle, and wide angle poses (second chakra); bow, boat, warrior one, warrior two, warrior three, sun salutation, and all twisting poses (third chakra); and bridge, child's, downward facing dog, shoulder stand, and standing half forward bend poses (sixth chakra) can help you connect with Empirista's energy.

EMPOWERISTA PROFILE

Definition: An Empowerista is a woman who creates and curates content, shares information and experiences, connects with others and establishes positive relationships, and builds and participates in communities that empower her and others.

Manifesto: I am a woman who lives fearlessly. I affirm and value relationships. I invest positive energy and time when I connect with others. I share information and experiences willingly in an effort to build community. I use my wisdom to guide me in how I affect the opinions and actions of others. I give birth to sisterhood through activism, connections, conversations, empowerment, and inspiration that transforms women's lives and communities.

Chakra Connection: Empowerista's energy is connected to the:

- Solar plexus, or third chakra, which corresponds to willpower, persistence, self-worth, self-confidence, and self-esteem. It governs the stomach, small intestine, liver, gallbladder, and spleen.
- Throat, or fifth chakra, which corresponds to communication, expressions of feelings, or the truth. It governs the throat, ears, nose, teeth, mouth, and neck.
- Third-eye, or sixth chakra, which corresponds to intuition, imagination, wisdom, and the ability to think and make decisions. It governs the eyes and base of the skull.

Color Connection: Wear or surround yourself with the colors yellow (third chakra), light or sky blue (fifth chakra), and indigo blue (sixth chakra) to connect with Empowerista's energy.

Gemstone Connection: Wear or surround yourself with citrine or tiger's eye (third chakra), turquoise (fifth chakra), and lapis lazuli (sixth chakra) gemstones to connect with Empowerista's energy.

Goddess Connection:

- Al-Uzza, the Arabian goddess of confidence, vigilance, and preparation; Amaterasu, the Japanese sun goddess of royal power; Durga, the Hindu warrior goddess; and Sekhmet, the Egyptian warrior goddess (third chakra)
- Vach, the Hindu goddess of speech and communication (fifth chakra)
- Tara, the Tibetan goddess of wisdom (sixth chakra)

Yoga Connection: Practicing bow, boat, warrior one, warrior two, warrior three, sun salutation, and all twisting poses (third chakra); bridge, fish, lion, plow, and upward plank poses (fifth chakra); and bridge, child's, downward facing dog, shoulder stand, and standing half forward bend poses (sixth chakra) can help you connect with Empowerista's energy.

ENCHANTISTA PROFILE

Definition: An Enchantista is a woman who taps into the magic of her spirit as she focuses her energy, opens her heart, trusts her intuition, embraces her fears, and shares her gifts in service to others.

Manifesto: I am a woman who believes life is a journey. I choose my true calling by being still and connecting with the spirit within. I allow grace and wisdom to permeate my inner sanctuary. They encourage me to surrender my ego and tap into my intuition. That's where the magic happens. I become my higher self. I celebrate who I am in this moment and who I am becoming in the next. Gratitude fills my heart because I know I am blessed.

Chakra Connection: Enchantista's energy is connected to the:

- Root, or first chakra, which corresponds to survival issues including food, shelter, money, and financial independence. It governs the feet, legs, bones, and spine.
- Sacral, or second chakra, which corresponds to creativity, pleasure, sexuality, and well-being. It governs the bladder, circulatory system, and sexual and reproductive organs.
- Solar plexus, or third chakra, which corresponds to willpower, persistence, self-worth, self-confidence, and self-esteem. It governs the stomach, small intestine, liver, gallbladder, and spleen.
- Heart, or fourth chakra, which corresponds to love, joy, harmony, and inner peace. It governs the heart, chest, lungs, and circulation).
- Throat, or fifth chakra, which corresponds to communication, expressions of feelings, or the truth. It governs the throat, ears, nose, teeth, mouth, and neck.
- Third-eye, or sixth chakra, which corresponds to intuition, imagination, wisdom, and the ability to think and make decisions. It governs the eyes and base of the skull.

- Crown, or seventh chakra, which corresponds to the crown of the head and pituitary gland. It governs the higher self or inner spirit.

Color Connection: Wear or surround yourself with the colors red (first chakra), orange (second chakra), yellow (third chakra), green or pink (fourth chakra), light or sky blue (fifth chakra), indigo blue (sixth chakra), and purple (seventh chakra) to connect with Enchantista's energy.

Gemstone Connection: Wear or surround yourself with garnet or ruby (first chakra), amber or carnelian (second chakra), citrine or tiger's eye (third chakra), aventurine or rose quartz (fourth chakra), turquoise (fifth chakra), lapis lazuli (sixth chakra), and amethyst (seventh chakra) gemstones to connect with Enchantista's energy.

Goddess Connection:

- Atira, the Pawnee Native American goddess of the earth; Coatlicue, the Mexican goddess of the earth; and Gaia, the Greek goddess of the earth (first chakra)
- Oshun, the Yoruba goddess of creativity, and Sarasvati, the Hindu goddess of the arts (second chakra)
- Al-Uzza, the Arabian goddess of confidence, vigilance, and preparation; Amaterasu, the Japanese sun goddess of royal power; Durga, the Hindu warrior goddess; and Sekhmet, the Egyptian warrior goddess (third chakra)
- Aphrodite, the Greek goddess of love; Erzulie, the Haitian goddess of love; Kwan Yin, the Chinese goddess of compassion; and Venus, the Roman goddess of love, (fourth chakra)
- Vach, the Hindu goddess of speech and communication (fifth chakra)
- Tara, the Tibetan goddess of wisdom (sixth chakra)

- Shakti, the Hindu goddess of divine feminine energy (seventh chakra)

Yoga Connection: Practicing mountain, warrior two, standing forward fold, and bridge poses (first chakra); bound angle, downward facing dog, triangle, and wide angle poses (second chakra); bow, boat, warrior one, warrior two, warrior three, sun salutation, and all twisting poses (third chakra); camel, cat, cobra, fish, sphinx, upward facing dog, and upward facing bow poses (fourth chakra); bridge, fish, lion, plow, and upward plank poses (fifth chakra); bridge, child's, downward facing dog, shoulder stand, and standing half forward bend poses (sixth chakra); and corpse, headstand, lotus, and half lotus poses (seventh chakra) can help you connect with Enchantista's energy.

EVANGELISTA PROFILE

Definition: An Evangelista is a woman who supports and advocates a philosophy, a values system, a lifestyle, a cause, or a campaign that improves her life and others' lives.

Manifesto: I am a woman who believes I can be heard, persuasive, enthusiastic, optimistic, passionate, articulate, generous, outgoing, and inspiring when I pursue what matters most. That's when I am a force. One for others. One for humanity. I am a voice for those who have no voice. The change maker. The advocate involved in supporting a great cause. A woman making a difference. A woman starting something good and helping the planet. A woman making the world a better place for all.

Chakra Connection: Evangelista's energy is connected to the:

- Sacral, or second chakra, which corresponds to creativity, pleasure, sexuality, and well-being. It governs the bladder, circulatory system, and sexual and reproductive organs.
- Solar plexus, or third chakra, which corresponds to willpower, persistence, self-worth, self-confidence, and self-esteem. It governs the stomach, small intestine, liver, gallbladder, and spleen.
- Heart, or fourth chakra, which corresponds to love, joy, harmony, and inner peace. It governs the heart, chest, lungs, and circulation).

Color Connection: Wear or surround yourself with the colors orange (second chakra), yellow (third chakra), and green or pink (fourth chakra) to connect with Evangelista's energy.

Gemstone Connection: Wear or surround yourself with amber or carnelian (second chakra), citrine or tiger's eye (third chakra), and aventurine or rose quartz (fourth chakra) gemstones to connect with Evangelista's energy.

Goddess Connection:

- Oshun, the Yoruba goddess of creativity, and Sarasvati, the Hindu goddess of the arts (second chakra)
- Al-Uzza, the Arabian goddess of confidence, vigilance, and preparation; Amaterasu, the Japanese sun goddess of royal power; Durga, the Hindu warrior goddess; and Sekhmet, the Egyptian warrior goddess (third chakra)
- Aphrodite, the Greek goddess of love; Erzulie, the Haitian goddess of love; Kwan Yin, the Chinese goddess of compassion; and Venus, the Roman goddess of love, (fourth chakra)

Yoga Connection: Practicing bound angle, downward facing dog, triangle, and wide angle poses (second chakra); bow, boat, warrior one, warrior two, warrior three, sun salutation, and all twisting poses (third chakra); and camel, cat, cobra, fish, sphinx, upward facing dog, and upward facing bow poses (fourth chakra) can help you connect with Evangelista's energy.

FLOWISTA PROFILE

Definition: A Flowista is a woman who unplugs from her digital life and tech devices for periods of time so she can recharge and take care of her own needs; and encourages women to unplug from their digital lives by incorporating mindfulness and self-care practices.

Manifesto: I am a woman who disconnects from her digital life and to-do list in order to find my flow and be present to what matters most in my life. When I unplug, I am giving myself the gift of self care. I am nurturing my spirit, mind, heart, and body. I am releasing stress and tension from all parts of my spirit, mind, heart, body, and life. I am creating space to relax, rest, and enjoy life. The end result is a healthier me.

Chakra Connection: Flowista's energy is connected to the:

- Throat, or fifth chakra, which corresponds to communication, expressions of feelings, or the truth. It governs the throat, ears, nose, teeth, mouth, and neck.
- Third-eye, or sixth chakra, which corresponds to intuition, imagination, wisdom, and the ability to think and make decisions. It governs the eyes and base of the skull.
- Crown, or seventh chakra, which corresponds to the crown of the head and pituitary gland. It governs the higher self or inner spirit.

Color Connection: Wear or surround yourself with the colors light or sky blue (fifth chakra), indigo blue (sixth chakra), and purple (seventh chakra) to connect with Flowista's energy.

Gemstone Connection: Wear or surround yourself with turquoise (fifth chakra), lapis lazuli (sixth chakra), and amethyst (seventh chakra) gemstones to connect with Flowista's energy.

Goddess Connection:

- Vach, the Hindu goddess of speech and communication (fifth chakra)
- Tara, the Tibetan goddess of wisdom (sixth chakra)
- Shakti, the Hindu goddess of divine feminine energy (seventh chakra)

Yoga Connection: Practicing bridge, fish, lion, plow, and upward plank poses (fifth chakra); bridge, child's, downward facing dog, shoulder stand, and standing half forward bend poses (sixth chakra); and corpse, headstand, lotus, and half lotus poses (seventh chakra) can help you connect with Flowista's energy.

LIFESTYLISTA PROFILE

Definition: A Lifestylista is a woman who lives her life as a work of art; expresses it through her passion for beauty, entertaining, fashion, food, home décor, personal style, and travel; and inspires others to live their lives as works of art.

Manifesto: I am a woman who lives her best life with passionate intention, purpose, and plenty of *joie de vivre*! In my heart of hearts, I know *la vie est belle*! I rejoice daily through an appreciation of all things beautiful. I celebrate by expressing my own beauty and style from the inside out. This energy inspires my home and office décor. It influences my taste buds and connects me to the pleasure of great food, wine, and dining experiences. It allows me to pursue and revel in the magnificence of the arts, culture, music, and travel adventures. It dazzles, shines, and sparkles in every facet of my life. So I let the good times roll!

Chakra Connection: Lifestylista's energy is connected to the:

- Sacral, or second chakra, which corresponds to creativity, pleasure, sexuality, and well-being. It governs the bladder, circulatory system, and sexual and reproductive organs.
- Solar plexus, or third chakra, which corresponds to willpower, persistence, self-worth, self-confidence, and self-esteem. It governs the stomach, small intestine, liver, gallbladder, and spleen.
- Heart, or fourth chakra, which corresponds to love, joy, harmony, and inner peace. It governs the heart, chest, lungs, and circulation).
- Throat, or fifth chakra, which corresponds to communication, expressions of feelings, or the truth. It governs the throat, ears, nose, teeth, mouth, and neck.

Color Connection: Wear or surround yourself with the colors orange (second chakra), yellow (third chakra), green or pink (fourth chakra), and light or sky blue (fifth chakra) to connect with Lifestylista's energy.

Gemstone Connection: Wear or surround yourself with amber or carnelian (second chakra), citrine or tiger's eye (third chakra), aventurine or rose quartz (fourth chakra), and turquoise (fifth chakra) gemstones to connect with Lifestylista's energy.
Goddess Connection:

- Oshun, the Yoruba goddess of creativity, and Sarasvati, the Hindu goddess of the arts (second chakra)
- Al-Uzza, the Arabian goddess of confidence, vigilance, and preparation; Amaterasu, the Japanese sun goddess of royal power; Durga, the Hindu warrior goddess; and Sekhmet, the Egyptian warrior goddess (third chakra)
- Aphrodite, the Greek goddess of love; Erzulie, the Haitian goddess of love; Kwan Yin, the Chinese goddess of compassion; and Venus, the Roman goddess of love, (fourth chakra)
- Vach, the Hindu goddess of speech and communication (fifth chakra)

Yoga Connection: Practicing bound angle, downward facing dog, triangle, and wide angle poses (second chakra); bow, boat, warrior one, warrior two, warrior three, sun salutation, and all twisting poses (third chakra); camel, cat, cobra, fish, sphinx, upward facing dog, and upward facing bow poses (fourth chakra); and bridge, fish, lion, plow, and upward plank poses (fifth chakra) can help you connect with Lifestylista's energy.

Digital Sisterhood Notes Section

Digital Sisterhood Notes Section

APPENDIX C

CREATE YOUR DIGITAL WELLNESS PLAN

This appendix includes an excerpt from my case study entitled "Lean In and Listen to Yourself" that was included in the 2012-2013 Hot Mommas Project case study library. Visit hotmommasproject.org. Tips from my BlogHer 2011 presentation on Blogger Wellness are also included.

My Digital Wellness Wake Up Call

Thirty-five years ago, I was 13 and reading Charlotte Bronte's novel, *Jane Eyre*. It was the summer before I entered the ninth grade at Elizabeth Seton High School, an all-girls Catholic school. *Jane Eyre* was required summer reading for Seton freshmen. After I checked the book out from the local library, I thought for sure it would take me a month to finish. I was so wrong. I devoured it in two weeks and managed to reread my favorite passages, which included a quote about courage: "I remember that the real world was wide, and that a varied field of hopes and fears, of sensations and excitements, awaited those who had courage to go forth into its expanse."

Bronte's wisdom on courage traveled with me throughout my four years at Seton. It taught me that having courage includes leaning in and listening to myself. As I have gotten older, I have allowed my life to travel at light speed online and offline, leaving little time to lean in and listen to myself on a regular basis. Twenty-first century living has convinced me I am supposed to be really busy with an assortment of electronic devices. It has exposed me to a myriad of choices and information. It has made my to-do list run wild with no end in sight. It has done all of these things only because I chose to allow it. The key phrase is "I CHOSE."

Two years ago, I started to realize how my choices to travel at light speed were burning me out. So I made a decision to slow down. Slowing down meant saying "NO" to activities, business opportunities, events, projects, and even some people. It meant reducing the time I spent with people, incorporating more time for meditation and yoga, and implementing a digital wellness plan that includes daily, weekly, and monthly periods of unplugging from my online life and electronic devices. Those changes weren't always welcomed by others. And some of them created a level of discomfort that left me feeling guilty. However, I used meditation and yoga to sit with the discomfort as I intentionally created more space in my life to lean in and listen to myself.

What I discovered was that I need time each day to be still and quiet. My meditation and yoga practices are the tools I use to achieve stillness so I can check in with my inner wisdom. Inner wisdom is often referred to as intuition or an inner voice that provides guidance. My intuition is my GPS for daily living. It helps me know and understand myself better. It fuels my courage and determination to follow my dreams. It allows me to express my authentic self.

Now that you know a little more about my decision to create and implement a digital wellness plan, it's time for you to explore several tips that can help you create your own plan.

Creating Your Digital Wellness Plan

A digital wellness plan is a gift you give yourself to help manage your time online with mindful self-care practices. Mindful self-care practices encourage you to slow down, become aware of how you spend your time online, and identify and take small steps towards having a healthier digital life. Examples include breathing exercises, journaling, massage, meditation, physical movement (walking, running, yoga, and aerobic classes), rest (naps and a good night's sleep), setting time boundaries, and using time management tools (HootSuite, TweetDeck, and an editorial calendar) to schedule your blog and social media posts.

- **TIP 1: BREATHE!**

Before you begin thinking about your digital wellness plan, find a comfortable seated position in your chair. Come to the edge of your chair and place your feet flat on the floor. If you are wearing glasses or shoes, take them off to relax. Create hip width distance in between your legs. Take a deep breath through your nose and exhale it through your mouth. Notice how you feel. Now do it SEVEN more times.

When you breathe intentionally and deeply, you invite yourself into the present moment. The more you breathe intentionally and deeply, the more open you become to PEACE. When you have PEACE, you are free to IMAGINE. Your imagination helps you DREAM. Your dreams help you CREATE and INSPIRE others in your blog, business, career, and family.

Four Takeaways from Breathing:

-Breathing creates Peace.
-Peace helps you Imagine.
-Your imagination helps you Dream.
-Your dreams help you Create and Inspire.

Breathing Exercise: Take SEVEN deep breaths. Inhale through your nose and exhale through your mouth to release any stress or pause any thoughts or to do lists you carried with you into this moment.

- **TIP 2: BREATHE AND WRITE WHY YOU NEED TO PRACTICE SELF CARE IN YOUR DIGITAL LIFE.**

Take SEVEN deep breaths. Inhale and exhale through your nose. Ask yourself why you need to practice self-care in your digital life. Use the next 10 to 20 minutes (or more if you need it) and a piece of paper, journal, smartphone, iPad, tablet, laptop, or desktop computer to write or type your response to the following writing prompt: "I need to practice self care in my digital life because _____ (fill in the blank)."

- **TIP 3: BREATHE AND WRITE WHAT YOU NEED TO PRACTICE SELF CARE IN YOUR DIGITAL LIFE.**

Take SEVEN deep breaths. Inhale and exhale through your nose. Ask yourself what you need in your digital life to practice self care. Use the next 10 to 20 minutes (or more if you need it) and a piece of paper, journal, smartphone, iPad, tablet, laptop, or desktop computer to write or type your response to the following writing prompt: "To practice self care in my digital life I need _____ (fill in the blank)."

Feel free to include the amount of time you need on a daily, weekly, monthly, or yearly basis to unplug. Consider taking sabbaticals or vacations from your digital life, too!

Share the types of activities you can do to rest, relax, and recharge.

Identify one or two people in your life that you can ask to be your accountability partner. An accountability partner is someone who will gently remind you to practice self care in your digital life.

If you can, give yourself a start date for launching your digital wellness plan.

- **TIP 4: IDENTIFY RESOURCES THAT CAN HELP YOU MAINTAIN YOUR DIGITAL WELLNESS PLAN.**

  - Digital Sisterhood Unplugged Weekend Resources, DigitalSisterhood.wordpress.com
  - *Digital Warriorship* by Gwen Bell (2012 Digital Sister of the Year—Flowista)
  - *Fast Company* #Unplug Guide, FastCompany.com/3012710/unplug
  - National Unplugged Day, SabbathManifesto.org/unplug
  - ReadySetPause.com
  - *The Digital Diet* by Daniel Sieberg

Just in case you need more suggestions for creating mini unplug moments, I have included a list of my favorites below:

- Before you get out of bed, incorporate breathing exercises into your morning routine by taking SEVEN deep breaths. Place your hand on your heart as you inhale and exhale through your nose.

- Establish FIVE minutes of "soothing your soul time" at the end of your day. UNPLUG from your electronic devices. Start with playing your favorite music. As you listen to the music, take SEVEN deep breaths. Inhale through your nose and exhale through your mouth. As you exhale, release any thoughts, stress, to do list items, or emotions that may prevent you from being in the present moment.

- While you're working during the day, UNPLUG from your electronic devices and take a THREE minute break by inhaling and exhaling through your nose three times.

- During your morning and evening commutes, UNPLUG from your digital devices and take FIVE deep breaths (inhale and exhale through your nose) before you turn your car or motorcycle/scooter, start to bike, or when you sit down on public transportation.

- Before answering your phone, take a deep breath (inhale and exhale through your nose).

My Final Thoughts

Remember to be patient with yourself as you make changes in your digital life. Take baby steps. Celebrate your victories, no matter how small or big they are. Use the Digital Sisterhood Notes Section to record your thoughts about your digital wellness plan. Enjoy your digital wellness journey!

Digital Sisterhood Notes Section

Digital Sisterhood Notes Section

APPENDIX D

Use Crowdfunding to Create, Build, and Fund Your Creative Projects, Entrepreneurial Endeavors, and Social Causes

Did you know women use social networking sites more than men? According to the Pew Research Center's Internet & American Life Project, 74% of women use social networking sites, compared with 62% of men in 2013. That 74% really excites me because it supports my belief that women are the perfect people to launch successful crowdfunding campaigns in the digital economy.

So what is crowdfunding? It is a web-based financial model that allows individuals to use social-networking sites to identify and solicit donors who pool their money in community to support creative projects, entrepreneurial endeavors, and social causes. There are four types of crowdfunding: donation-based, equity-based, lending-based, and reward-based. Donation-based crowdfunding allows you to give a financial contribution to a charitable cause. With reward-based crowdfunding, you invest a certain financial amount and receive a reward which is a tangible item or service in return for your investment. Equity-based crowdfunding offers you a stake in the company when you make a financial investment. Lending-based crowdfunding treats your financial contribution as a loan that will be repaid over a period of time. For purposes of this Appendix, the information I am sharing relates primarily to donation and rewards-based crowdfunding.

Overview of Crowdfunding Platforms
Three of the most popular rewards-based crowdfunding platforms are GoFundMe, Indiegogo, and Kickstarter. PayPal is another web platform people use to collect donations.

- GoFundMe.com
- Indiegogo.com (co-founded by a female entrepreneur Danae Ringelmann)
- Kickstarter.com (nonprofit organizations cannot use the platform)
- PayPal.com

There are other crowdfunding platforms and online fundraising web sites that support children and youth, ethnic groups, nonprofit organizations, social causes, and women. See the list below.

Children and Youth
- Piggybackr.com is a crowdfunding platform that helps children and youth (kindergarten through college-aged kids) to raise money for their specific cause (co-founded by female entrepreneur Andrea Lo).

Ethnic Groups
- Aflamnah.com is the first crowdfunding platform dedicated to helping independent filmmakers, artists, geeks, students, innovators, and thinkers in the Arab world raise funds for their projects (co-founded by female entrepreneur Vida Rizq).
- BlackStartUp.com is a crowdfunding platform for projects and ideas that will have a positive impact on the African American community.
- Crowdismo.com is a Latino crowdfunding platform that Latino entrepreneurs, designers, programmers, marketers,

educators, students, community leaders, cause champions, journalists, engineers, inventors, artists, and producers can use to fund their projects.

- ShopZAOZAO.com is a crowdfunding platform that allows Asian designers to post projects and receive production funding (founded by female entrepreneurs Ling Cai and Vicky Wu).

Nonprofit Organizations and Social Causes

- Crowdrise.com is an online fundraising web site that allows individual fundraisers, nonprofit fundraising, and event fundraising (co-founded by female film producer Shauna Robertson).
- Fundly.com is a social fundraising platform that helps individuals and organizations raise money for causes they care about.
- GiveForward.com is an online fundraising web site that allows friends and family to donate to patients navigating a medical crisis (co-founded by female entrepreneur Desiree Vargas Wrigley).
- Razoo.com is a crowdfunding platform for causes.

Women

- Catapalt.org is a crowdfunding site that works for gender justice and equality that only nonprofit and charitable organizations can use (co-founded by female entrepreneur Maz Kessler).
- CrowdHelps.com is a crowdfunding platform that helps women. People can help change a woman's life by donating funds, professional advice, free time, or kind words (co-founded by female entrepreneur Silvia Podubni).
- GirlTank.org is a community and crowdfunding platform that helps women and girl changemakers fund and grow their social enterprises (founded by female entrepreneurs Tara Roberts and Sejal Hathis).

- Moola-Hoop.com is a crowdfunding platform for women entrepreneurs, owners, and managers (founded by female entrepreneurs Brenda Bazan and Nancy Hayes).
- NapTimeStartUps.com is a crowdfunding web site for mom and women entrepreneurs that will launch in December 2013 (founded by female entrepreneurs Catherine Snowman and Jenivieve Elly).

If you are raising money for your film or online television program and looking for an alternative to Indiegogo and Kickstarter (two of the most popular platforms for filmmakers and webisode creators), check out the following platforms.

- JuntoBoxFilms.com is a film collaboration and mentoring studio that uses its social platform to empower creators, writers, producers, directors, and actors to develop films with budgets starting at $250,000.
- Mobcaster.com is a crowdfunding platform focused on finding, funding, and broadcasting independent online television programs.
- SeedandSpark.com is a selective film crowdfunding platform that approves each project (founded by female entrepreneur and filmmaker Emily Seed).
- Slated.com is an online film marketplace that connects a network of investors, filmmakers, and industry professionals.

For more resources, see the information below:
- Ananda's Crowdfunding Pinterest Board, pinterest.com/anandaleeke/crowdfunding
- *Crowdfunding: How to Run a Successful Crowdfunding Campaign* by Jane Monica-Jones
- *Indiegogo Field Guide by Indiegogo*, http://landing.indiegogo.com/iggfieldguide (free to download)
- *Crowdfunding for Filmmakers* by John T. Trigonis
- *Kickstarter for Dummies* by Aimee Cebulski

- Ian MacKenzie's Crowdfunding Resources, ianmack.com/crowdfunding-web/crowdfunding
- National Crowdfunding Association, NLCFA.org
- *Successfully Crowdfund Your Dream Idea on Kickstarter* by Natalie Sisson
- *The Everything Guide to Crowdfunding* by Thomas Elliott Young

My Kickstarter Crowdfunding Experience

My crowdfunding journey began with a challenge from my financial advisor Judy Weathers during our first quarter meeting in 2010. Judy and I were reviewing my self-publishing expenses for two books published in 2007 and 2009, and estimating the expenses for a third book (the one you are reading now). She asked me if I could find investors or alternative funding for the book. At first, I thought she was asking me to do the impossible, but a small voice inside convinced me to be open and pursue alternative funding.

Months passed without me lifting a finger to identify alternative funding. Then, it happened. The light bulb went off during an episode of Digital Sisterhood Radio. I was moderating a panel of creative women in social media when Abiola Abrams, author and founder of AbiolaTV.com, referenced an *Essence* article that discussed the power of using Kickstarter to fund books and films. After the show, I visited Kickstarter.com and learned about several authors who used it to raise money for their books. Their success inspired me to take the plunge.

Here's what happened: I created two Kickstarter campaigns for my self-publishing package and photography fees. Using video was a must for me. So I recorded an eight-minute video with my laptop's web cam that was very simple and shared my reasons for writing the book and using Kickstarter. I included the same information in the description section of my campaign page. I also offered seven pledge options ($1, $5, $10, $20, $50, $100, and $200) with rewards that included:

- $1Pledge: Donors names will be published in the book as supporters.

- $5 Pledge: Donors will receive everything mentioned above and access to the behind-the-scenes video & audio updates that will document the creation of the book.

- $10 Pledge: Donors will receive everything mentioned above and access to a live author chat on UStream.tv during the book writing and publishing process.

- $20 Pledge: Donors will receive everything mentioned above, a personal thank—you note with book logo and signed by author, and an invitation to participate in the online book release party via UStream.tv.

- $50 Pledge: Donors will receive everything mentioned above, an invitation to vote on the book cover design, and a Digital Sisterhood mug.

- $100 Pledge: Donors will receive everything mentioned above and an autographed copy of the book.

- $200 Pledge: Donors will receive everything mentioned above and a private one-hour author chat via Skype or telephone with the author.

With the support of my generous donors (backers is the Kickstarter term), my first campaign raised $1,159 in 2010. My second campaign raised $701 in 2011. I also received donations via PayPal and from friends who gave me cash and check donations.

My funding goals were very conservative. I wanted to make sure I received every dollar I raised because Kickstarter only offers fixed funding, an all-or-nothing approach. That means if you don't reach your funding goal, you don't receive any of the money you raised.

The biggest challenges I faced with my campaigns were writing a book while I was conducting two fundraisers and underestimating the time it would actually take to publish the book. My underestimation caused a three-year delay in my delivery of rewards to my donors. To maintain communication with my donors, I posted regular updates about my writing process in 2011 and part of 2012. I slacked off in 2013. Fortunately, my donors have not complained. They are a great group of people who have a lot of compassion and patience. They taught me that crowdfunding is rooted in generosity. For that, I am truly grateful.

As a result of my experience, I believe crowdfunding is rooted in:

- Passion for a cause, project, or venture;
- The experience of connection, relationship building, and social capital within a community;
- The power of asking;
- The act of generosity; and
- The practice of gratitude.

Now that you know more about crowdfunding and my journey, I thought you might like a checklist to help guide you through the process of developing your own campaign. I created it based on my experience and coaching work with creative professionals and organizations that are using crowdfunding.

Crowdfunding Campaign Plan Checklist

❖ PROJECT DESCRIPTION: Describe your crowdfunding project in 140 characters or less. Give it a name that sparks interest. You will be able to use this short description as a springboard for writing your full campaign description (narrative or story).

❖ FUNDING GOAL: How much money do you want to raise?

❖ FUNDING PLEDGES: What types of pledges are you seeking to receive from donors ($1, $5, $10, $20, $30, $40, $50, $75, $100, $200 or more)?

❖ CROWDFUNDING MODEL: What type of crowdfunding model works best for your project: fixed funding or flexible funding?

❖ CROWDFUNDING PLATFORM: What crowdfunding platforms are best suited for your project (GoFundMe, Indiegogo, Kickstarter or others)?

❖ CROWDFUNDING PROJECT BEST PRACTICES: Identify five or more examples of similar crowdfunding projects. Watch the campaign videos. Read the campaign descriptions. Check out the pledge amounts and types of rewards. Review any updates that were sent to donors. Take notes on what you like or dislike.

❖ CAMPAIGN LAUNCH DATE: When will you launch the crowdfunding campaign?

- Can your launch date be tied to a major awareness event or during a month when you think your audience will be more interested in supporting you?

- Will you launch the campaign with a special online event (Google+ Hangout video chat or Twitter chat) or offline event (meet up)?

❖ DURATION OF CAMPAIGN: How long will you run the campaign (number of days you will use to raise the funding)?

❖ CAMPAIGN TEAM: Who will help you manage the campaign (interns, social media enthusiasts, marketing/PR professionals or volunteers, family members, and friends)?

❖ CAMPAIGN COMMUNITY (AMBASSADORS AND DONORS): Who are the members of your campaign community?

- Make a list (use an Excel spreadsheet) of your blog readers, email list members, e-newsletter subscribers, Facebook fans, friends, and group members, Google+ friends, Instagram followers, LinkedIn members, Pinterest followers, Twitter followers, and YouTube and Vimeo subscribers, and other social networking site friends.

- What organizations and groups do you belong to? Do you have the contact information for the organizers and the group members?

- What conferences or events do you regularly attend? Do you have the contact information for the organizers and the people you have met at the events?

- What groups of people will be interested in your campaign? Do you have the contact information for the groups (web site, email address, Facebook, Google+, LinkedIn, Twitter, and other sites)?

- Your campaign community members are your donor base. Ask them to donate to your campaign.

- Your campaign community members are also your potential ambassadors for your campaign. Ask them to share your campaign information, social media, and video with people in their online, email, and offline networks.

❖ YOUR CROWDFUNDING CAMPAIGN FULL DESCRIPTION: Why is your campaign project needed? How will your campaign project make the world better? What makes you the person to lead your campaign project? How do you plan to spend the money once you have raised it?

❖ CAMPAIGN REWARDS: How will you thank your ambassadors and donors for supporting your campaign? What rewards will you offer your donors?

- Research the rewards offered by other crowdfunding campaigns.
- Develop a list of 10 creative and personal rewards you can offer.
- How much money will it cost you to deliver the rewards (factor in shipping and packaging fees)?

❖ CAMPAIGN COMMUNICATION AND OUTREACH STRATEGIES: What tools will you use to communicate with your audience? Are you going to create a video or use any photos (I say DO BOTH!)?

- Identify where your audience members spend their time online. Hopefully, you have established an online presence on the sites.

- Use Facebook, Google+, Instagram, LinkedIn, Pinterest (create a board for your campaign), Tumblr, Twitter, Vimeo, and YouTube to promote your campaign, drum up positive media coverage from bloggers/e-zines/magazines/newspapers, and recruit new campaign community members (ambassadors and donors).

- Brainstorm ideas for your videos. How will you make your videos (web cam flip camera, phone camera)? Where will you record the videos? Who will help you make the videos? Will you use any music or photos in the videos?

You may want to do three short videos (one to three minutes) during the campaign. The first video could be used as your pitch video (two to three minutes). Your pitch video tells your story. Watch five to seven pitch videos created for successful campaigns. Make note of why you like them. Try to incorporate some of their best features in your video.

The second video (one to two minutes) could be a status update about the campaign which includes shout outs to campaign ambassadors and donors (one to two minutes).

The third video could be a final thank you to your supporters.

- You may want to prepare a short script for your videos. Keep your script simple and easy to understand. Practice what you will say several times. Record three sample videos and ask several people to critique your presentation.

- When you record your video, make sure you wear clothing (and hairstyle and make up) that compliments you. You want to look relaxed, down-to-earth, and friendly. Have fun!

- Create an editorial calendar and sample posts that you will use throughout the campaign. Include dates for submitting press releases about the campaign (status updates with any successes).

- To make the lives of your campaign ambassadors easier, send them sample posts or tweets that they can share with their networks.

❖ ADDITIONAL CAMPAIGN FUNDING SOURCES: Will you use PayPal.com to collect donations from donors who may not want to use your crowdfunding platform? Will you accept cash and personal checks from donors who may not want to use PayPal.com or your crowdfunding platform?

❖ CELEBRATING YOUR CAMPAIGN SUCCESS: How will you celebrate your campaign's success? Will you host an online event (Twitter chat or Google+ Hangout) or a local event (open house, meet up or happy hour) in your city or town? Will you send a video thank you, email thank-you notes, or mail personalized thank you notes?

❖ POST CAMPAIGN OUTREACH: How will you keep in touch with your campaign community of ambassadors, donors, and supporters? Will you send them monthly or quarterly updates via email or an e-newsletter? Will you post a series of updates on your campaign update page, blog, or Facebook page?

Digital Sisterhood Notes Section

Digital Sisterhood Notes Section

APPENDIX E

Book Resources

1. Blogging
   - *Angel's Laws of Blogging: What You Need to Know If You Want to Have a Successful and Profitable Blog* by Angel Laws
   - *Blog Inc.: Blogging for Passion, Profit, and to Create Community* by Joy Deangdeelert Cho
   - *Blogalicious Savvy Social Media Guide: Running a Blog As a Business* by Shannon Nash
   - *Blogalicious Savvy Social Media Guide: Totally Rockin' the World with Your Niche Blog* by Amy Mascott
   - *Blogging for Bliss: Crafting Your Own Online Journal* by Tara Frey
   - *Blogging for Creatives* by Robin Houghton
   - *Blogging with Moxie* by Joelle Reeder and Katherine Scoleri
   - *Blogging Your Way to the Front Row* by Yuli Ziv
   - *5 Ways to {Blank} Your Blog* by Deb Rox
   - *No One Cares What You Had for Lunch: 100 Ideas for Your Blog* by Margaret Mason
   - *The Huffington Post Complete Guide to Blogging* by the Editors of the Huffington Post

2. Branding, Business, Career Reinvention, and Crowdfunding
   - *Craving Success: A Startup Junkie's Path from Passion to Profits* by Melody Biringer
   - *Crowdfunding: How to Run a Successful Crowdfunding Campaign* by Jane Monica-Jones

- *Enchantment: The Art of Changing Hearts, Minds, and Actions* by Guy Kawasaki
- *Entrepreneur's Manifesto* by Alli Worthington
- *Flipped It!—Inspiring Stories of Success Reinvention* by Melody Biringer
- *How She Got Free: A 5-Step Spiritual Business Manual for Women Who Lead Through Entrepreneurship* by Katrina M. Harrell and Akilah S. Richards
- *Me 2.0: Build A Powerful Brand to Achieve Career Success* by Dan Schawbel
- *MORE Magazine 287 Secrets of Reinventing Your Life: Big and Small Ways to Embrace New Possibilities* by MORE Magazine
- *101 Ways to Build a Powerful Personal Brand Inside and* Out by Liz Dennery Sanders
- *115 PR Tips to Brand Your Ministry* by Pam Perry
- *Online Success Guide* by Alli Worthington
- *Rework* by Jason Fried and David Heinemeier Hansson
- *She Takes on the World: A Guide to Being Your Own Boss, Working Happy, and Living on Purpose* by Natalie MacNeil
- *Start Your Business* by Alli Worthington
- *Successful Women Think Differently* by Valorie Burton
- *Successfully Crowdfund Your Dream Idea on Kickstarter* by Natalie Sisson
- *The Suitcase Entrepreneur: Create freedom in business and adventure in life* by Natalie Sisson
- *The Brand YU Life: Re-Thinking Who You Are Through Personal Brand Management* by Hajj E. Flemings
- *The Definitive List of Tools to Run Your Business from Anywhere* by Natalie Sisson
- *The Jet Set Girl's Guide to Building A Million-Dollar Online Empire* by Cheryl Broussard
- *The Mocha Manual to Turning Your Passion into Profit: How to Find and Grow Your Hustle in Any Economy* by Kimberly Seals-Allers
- *The Right Brain Business Plan: A Creative, Visual Map for Success* by Jennifer Lee

- *Trust Agents: Using the Web to Build Influence, Improve Reputation, and Earn Trust* by Chris Brogan and Julien Smith
- *25 Incredible Lessons Learned from Being in Business* by Natalie Sission

3. Creativity
   - *Artists' Journals and Sketchbooks: Exploring and Creating Personal Pages* by Lynne Perrella
   - *Chicana Art* by Laura E. Perez
   - *Collage Discovery Workshop: Beyond the Unexpected* by Claudine Hellmuth
   - *Collage for the Soul: Expressing Hopes and Dreams Through Art* by Holly Harrison and Paula Grasdal
   - *Coming Out The Wilderness: A Memoir of A Black Woman Artist* by Estella Conwill Majozo
   - *Create Dangerously: The Immigrant Artist at Work* by Edwidge Danticat
   - *Making Your Creative Mark* by Eric Maisel
   - *Taking Flight: Inspiration and Techniques to Give Your Creative Spirit Wings* by Kelly Rae Roberts
   - *The Artist's Way: A Spiritual Path to Higher Creativity* by Julia Cameron
   - *The Diary of Frida Kahlo: An Intimate Self-Portrait* by Carlos Fuentes and Sarah M. Lowe
   - *The 12 Secrets of Highly Creative Women: A Portable Mentor* by Gail McMeekin
   - *The Well of Creativity* edited by Michael Toms
   - *We Flew over the Bridge: The Memoirs of Faith Ringgold* by Faith Ringgold

4. Digital Age, Civility, and Engagement
   - *Civility in the Digital Age: How Companies and People Can Triumph over Haters, Trolls, Bullies, and Other Jerks* by Andrea Weckerle
   - *Release 2.1: A Design for Living in the Digital Age* by Esther Dyson

- *Social Change Any Time Everywhere: How to Implement Online Multichannel Strategies to Spark Advocacy, Raise Money, and Engage Your Community* by Allyson Kapin and Amy Sample Ward

5. Feminism and Women's Issues
   - *Cybergrrl!: A Woman's Guide to the World Wide Web* by Aliza Sherman
   - *Feminism Is for Everybody* by bell hooks
   - *Havana Real: One Woman Fights to Tell the Truth About Cuba Today* by Yoani Sanchez
   - *Kirsy Takes A Bow: A Celebration of Women's Favorites Online* edited by Laura Mayes
   - *PunditMom's Mothers of Intention: How Women & Social Media Are Revolutionizing Politics in America* by Joanne Bamberger
   - *Sistah Vegan: Black Female Vegans Speak on Food, Identity, Health, and Society* by A. Breeze Harper
   - *To Be Real: Telling the Truth and Changing the Face of Feminism* edited by Rebecca Walker

6. Lifestyle, Living Well, and Personal Development
   - *A Course in Miracles* by Foundation for Inner Peace
   - *A Return to Love: Reflections on the Principles of a Course in Miracles* by Marianne
   - *A Woman's Worth* by Marianne Williamson
   - *Archetypes: Who Are You* by Caroline Myss
   - *Encyclopedia of Goddesses and Heroines* by Patricia Monaghan
   - *Execumama Survival Kit* by Akilah S. Richards
   - *40 Days to Power Living: Think, Eat & Live on Purpose* by Teresa Kay-Aba Kennedy
   - *Fortytude: Making the Next Decades the Best Years of Your Life—through the 40s, 50s, and Beyond* by Sarah Brokaw
   - *Get Yours!: How to Have Everything You Ever Dreamed of and More* by Amy DuBois Barnett

- *Goddess in Everywoman: Powerful Archetypes in Women's Lives* by Jean Shinoda Bolen
- *Good Self, Bad Self: Transforming Your Worst Qualities into Your Biggest Assets* by Judy Smith
- *Having It All?: Black Women and Success* by Veronica Chambers
- *How to Be: A Guide to Contemporary Living for African Americans* by Harriette Cole
- *In the Spirit* by Susan L. Taylor
- *Lean In: Women, Work, and the Will to Lead* by Sheryl Sandberg
- *Lessons in Living* by Susan L. Taylor
- *Life Design 101* by Akilah S. Richards
- *Mad at Mile: A Black Woman's Guide to Truth* by Pearl Cleage
- *Madly in Love with Me: The Daring Adventure of Becoming Your Own Best Friend* by Christine Arylo
- *More Than Serving Tea: Asian American Women on Expectations, Relationships, Leadership, and Faith* by Asifa Dean, Christie Heller de Leon, Kathy Khang, and Nikki A. Toyama
- *On Becoming Fearless* by Arianna Huffington
- *Outliers: The Story of Success* by Malcolm Gladwell
- *Path Finder: A Course in Finding Your Own Beautiful Different* by Karen Walrond
- *Sacred Contracts* by Caroline Myss
- *Sacred Woman: A Guide to Healing the Feminine Body, Mind, and Spirit* by Queen Afua
- *Sisters of the Yam: Black Women and Self-Recovery* by bell hooks
- *The Book of Latina Women: 150 Vidas of Passion, Strength, and Success* by Sylvia Mendoza
- *Tapping the Power Within: A Path of Self-Empowerment for Women* by Iyanla Vanzant
- *The Beauty of Different* by Karen Walrond
- *The Declaration of You* by Jessica Swift and Michelle Ward

- *The Digital Diet: The 4-Step Plan to Break Your Tech Addiction and Regain Balance in Your Life* by Daniel Sieberg
- *The Fire Starter Sessions: A Soulful & Practical Guide to Creating Success on Your Own Terms* by Danielle LaPorte
- *The Goddess Path: Myths, Invocations, and Rituals* by Patricia Monaghan
- *The Gifts of Imperfection* by Brene Brown
- *The Joy of Doing Things Badly: A Girl's Guide to Love, Life, and Foolish Bravery* by Veronica Chambers
- *The Way of the Happy Woman: Living the Best Year of Your Life* by Sara Avant Stover
- *The Wisdom of Menopause: Creating Physical and Emotional Health During the Change* by Christine Northrup
- *The Tranquility du Jour Daybook* by Kimberly Wilson
- *Tranquilista: Mastering the Art of Enlightened Work and Mindful Play* by Kimberly Wilson
- *Tranquilologie: A DIY Guide to Everyday Tranquility* by Kimberly Wilson
- *Women's Bodies, Women's Wisdom* by Christine Northrup
- *You Can Heal Your Life* by Louise L. Hay
- *Your Inner Eve: discovering God's Woman Within* by Susan Newman

7. Personal Finance
   - *A Purse of Your Own!: An Easy Guide to Financial Security* by Deborah Owens
   - *The Energy of Money: A Spiritual Guide to Financial and Personal Fulfillment* by Maria Nemeth
   - *The Frugalista Files: How One Woman Got Out of Debt Without Giving Up the Fabulous Life* by Natalie McNeal
   - *The Law of Money of Divine Compensation: On Work, Money, and Miracles* by Marianne Williamson
   - *The 9 Steps to Financial Freedom* by Suze Orman
   - *Women & Money: Owning the Power to Control Your Destiny* by Suze Orman

- *You've Earned It, Don't Lose It: Mistakes You Can't Afford to Make When You Retire* by Suze Orman and Linda Mead

8. Social Media, Marketing, and Networking
   - *Black Women Online* by LaShanda Henry
   - *Create Your Own Ningalicious Network* by LaShanda Henry
   - *Internet Marketing Power* by LaShanda Henry
   - *Renegades Write the Rules: How the Digital Royalty Use Social Media to Innovate* by Amy Jo Martin
   - *Share This!: How You Will Change the World with Social Networking* by Deanna Zandt
   - *Social Media Engagement for Dummies* by Aliza Sherman and Danielle Elliott Smith
   - *Social Media 101* by Chris Brogan
   - *Social Media for Social Good* by Heather Mansfield
   - *Social Media Tactics for Nonprofits* by Melanie Mathos and Chad Norman
   - *The Complete Idiot's Guide to Crowdsourcing* by Aliza Sherman
   - *The Everything Blogging Book: Publish Your Ideas, Get Feedback, and Create Your Own Worldwide Network* by Aliza Sherman
   - *The New Community Rules: Marketing on the Social Web* by Tamar Weinberg
   - *The Networked Nonprofit* by Allison H. Fine and Beth Kanter
   - *The Whuffie Factor: Using the Power of Social Networks to Build Your Business* by Tara Hunt

9. Style
   - *Before You Put That On: 365 Daily Style Tips for Her* by Lloyd Boston
   - *Commander in Chic: Every Woman's Guide to Managing Her Style Like a First Lady* by Mikki Taylor
   - *Effortless Style* by June Ambrose
   - *How to Be a Budget Fashionista: The Ultimate Guide to Looking Fabulous for Less* by Kathryn Finney

- *Never Pay Retail Again: Shop Smart, Spend Less, and Look Your Best Ever* by Daisy Lewellyn
- *The Little Black Book of Style* by Nina Garcia
- *What I Wore: Four Seasons, One Closet, Endless Recipes for Personal Style* by Jessica Quirk

10. Writing
   - *APE: Author, Publisher, Entrepreneur: How to Publish a Book* by Guy Kawasaki
   - *Living Out Loud: A Writer's Journey* by Marita Golden
   - *Remembered Rapture: The Writer at Work* by bell hooks
   - *The Right to Write: An Invitation and Initiation into the Writing Life* by Julia Cameron
   - *The True Secret of Writing: Connecting Life with Language* by Natalie Goldberg
   - *The Yahoo! Style Guide: The Ultimate Sourcebook for Writing, Editing, and Creating Content for the Digital World* by Chris Barr and the Senior Editors of Yahoo!
   - *Writing Down the Bones: Freeing the Writer Within* by Natalie Goldberg
   - *Writing What You Know* by Marion Roach Smith
   - *Writing the Fire: Yoga and the Art of Making Your Words Come Alive* by Gail Sher
   - *Writing the Memoir* by Judith Barrington

11. Yoga, Chakras, and Spirituality
   - *Awakening Shakti: The Transformative Power of the Goddesses of Yoga* by Sally Kempton
   - *Chakra Mantras: Liberate Your Spiritual Genius Through Chanting* by Thomas Ashley-Farrand
   - *Confirmation: The Spiritual Wisdom That Has Shaped Our Lives* by Khephra Burns and Susan L. Taylor
   - *Essential Reiki: A Complete Guide to An Ancient Healing Art* by Diane Stein
   - *Healing Mantras: Using Sound Affirmations for Personal Power, Creativity, and Healing* by Thomas Ashley-Farrand

- *Hip Tranquil Chick: A Guide to Life On and Off the Yoga Mat* by Kimberly Wilson
- *Hormone Balance Through Yoga: A Pocket Guide for Women Over 40* by Claudia Turske
- *May I Be Happy: A Memoir of Love, Yoga, and Changing My Mind* by Cyndi Lee
- *Mudras: Yoga in Your Hands* by Gertrud Hirschi
- *OM Yoga: A Guide to Daily Practice* by Cyndi Lee
- *Opening to Spirit: Contacting the Healing Power of the Chakras & Honouring African Spirituality* by Caroline Shola Arewa
- *Shakti Mantras* by Thomas Ashley-Farrand
- *The Book of Chakra Healing* by Liz Simpson
- *The Secret Power of Yoga: A Woman's Guide to the Heart and Spirit of the Yoga Sutras* by Nischala Joy Devi
- *The Women's Health Big Book of Yoga* by Kathryn Budig
- *The Yin Yoga Kit: The Practice of Quiet Power* by Biff Mithoefer
- *Yin Sights: A Journey into the Philosophy & Practice of Yin Yoga* by Bernie Clark
- *Yin Yoga: Outline of A Quiet Practice* by Paul Grilley
- *Yoga and the Wisdom of Menopause: A Guide to Physical, Emotional, and Spiritual Health at Midlife and Beyond* by Suza Francina
- *Yoga for Suits: 30 No-Sweat Power Poses to Do in Pinstripes* by Edward Vilga
- *Yoga in Bed: 20 Asanas to Do in Pajamas* by Edward Vilga
- *Yogini: The Power of Women in Yoga* by Janice Gates

Ananda Kiamsha Madelyn Leeke

Digital Sisterhood Notes Section

Digital Sisterhood Notes Section

APPENDIX F

DIGITAL SISTERHOOD MILESTONES

Digital Sisterhood Milestones are significant moments in your online life that inspire you to dream bigger, help you grow and learn, connect you to others, and offer opportunities to share information, expertise, and experiences with others. Each year, I make a list of my milestones. See below (it is pretty long—so get a cup of something yummy to sip and read on!).

The list helps me chart my own growth. It also helps me identify digital diva sheroes, virtual mentors, ideas, and resources I may have forgotten about. Most importantly, it encourages me to celebrate my accomplishments and discoveries. Feel free to use the Digital Sisterhood Notes Section to make a list of your own milestones.

My Digital Sisterhood Milestones include:

❖ 1995
- Visiting the Internet café at the United Nations Fourth World Conference on Women in Beijing, China and realizing the power women have when they gain access to the web, and signing up for my first AOL email account after returning home.
- Discovering Candace Carpenter's iVillage online community for women.

❖ 1996
- Working as a knowledge manager for *e.villages,* an information technology company that provided database

services to U.S. Government agencies and the healthcare industry, and hired residents of low-income, underserved communities.

❖ 1997
  • Serving as an intellectual property protection manager for digital products and services at the Hamilton Securities Group, Inc.
  • Falling head over hills in love with Oprah Winfrey's web site.

❖ 1998
  • Witnessing Esther Dyson named the founding chairman of the Internet Corporation for Assigned Names and Numbers.
  • Creating my first electronic newsletter Walk in the Electronic Light Ministry.

❖ 1999
  • Serving as a contributing writer for NetNoir.com's Gospel and Women's Channels.

❖ 2000
  • Joining Cheryl Mayberry McKissack's NiaOnline.com community for African American women.
  • Learning about Shireen Mitchell's Digital Sisters, a nonprofit organization which focuses on using digital media and technology for women and diverse communities.
  • Hosting the launch party of Kiamsha.com, my first web site that featured my art, poetry, and creative writing, at the CyberStop Café.

❖ 2001
  • Discovering Smith Center for Healing and the Arts web site, connecting via email with Smith Center's executive director Shanti Norris, and meeting with Shanti to finalize my role as a Smith Center artist-in-residence.

- Tracking the success of Lynne Johnson's digital career and life through LynnedJohnson.com.

❖ 2005
- Launching my first author blog on Blogger.com.

❖ 2006
- Creating my yoga blog on Blogger.com to market my services as a yoga teacher and Reiki practitioner.
- Joining Myspace and connecting with London-based writers, artists, spoken word performers, and musicians to help develop dialogue for my novel, *Love's Troubadours: Karma—Book One*'s British characters.

❖ 2007
- Traveling to London to do research for *Love's Troubadours* and meeting Natalie Lue, founder of Baggage Reclaim blog.
- Becoming an active member of the Black Author Showcase social networking site.
- Hosting my first online book party for my novel, *Love's Troubadours* with a YouTube video on Myspace and my author blog.
- Launching my yoga Meetup.com group to build an online community of D.C. yoga practitioners who meet offline to practice kind and gentle yoga for social good causes and health awareness campaigns in Malcolm X—Meridian Hill Park during the Spring, Summer, and Fall seasons.
- Developing a digital addiction to Angela Benton's Black Web 2.0, the premier destination for African Americans in technology and new media, and Deanna Sutton's *Clutch Magazine*, an online women's lifestyle publication.

❖ 2008
- Using Ning.com to build BAP Living, a social networking site for women of African descent who self-identified with my *Love's Troubadours*' main character, Karma Francois,

a Black American Princess; and Go Green Sangha, a social networking site for creative professionals who practice green living, creativity, yoga, meditation, and the healing arts.

- Getting my soul fed while reading the Kitchen Table blog on race, politics, religion, and popular culture published by Professors Melissa Harris-Perry and Yolanda Pierce.
- Tuning into Kimberly Wilson's Tranquility du Jour podcast for a weekly dose of creative and yoga inspiration.
- Being interviewed as the February Member of the Month on the Black Author Showcase Talkshoe.com radio show.
- Developing a regular art-making practice by participating in Leah Piken Kolidas's Art Every Day Month online challenge.

❖ 2009
- Practicing yoga with Faith Hunter Yoga's All the Way Live podcasts.
- Being a part of the first-ever Feminism 2.0 Conference, Blogalicious Weekend Conference, She's Geeky DC Unconference, and Latinos in Social Media DC Conference.
- Interviewing women in social media I met at blogging conferences and meet ups on my Talkshoe.com radio show and YouTube channel.
- Joining SheWrites.com, an online community for women writers.
- Using Ustream.tv to live stream a series of author talks to support my online book party for my creative memoir, *That Which Awakens Me.*
- Staying updated on social media by reading Corvida Raven's SheGeeks.Net, a technology blog written in plain English.
- Improving my social media "A" game by reading Deb Rox's *Five Ways to Blank Your Blog* and Tara Hunt's *The Whuffie Factor.*
- Finding my creative tribe of women by participating in Jamie Ridler's Next Chapter Book Blog Group.

❖ 2010

- Volunteering to build a Twitter directory and to record video interviews of technology volunteers during CrisisCamp DC's Chile earthquake disaster relief efforts held at the World Bank.
- Watching Carmen Elana Mitchell's "The Real Girl's Guide to Everything Else," a comedy webisodes series; Toni Odom's "AHSHE," a soap opera webisodes series; and Sonya Steele's webisodes series "Celeste Bright."
- Gaining social media wisdom as I read Deanna Zandt's *Share This!* And Beth Kanter and Alison Fine's *The Networked Nonprofit.*
- Deepening my work as a yoga teacher, creativity coach, and Reiki Master practitioner by reading Yael Flusberg's Y's Elements blog that chronicles the wise elements of transformative practices including yoga, Reiki, meditation, coaching, writing, and organizational development.
- Live blogging President Barack Obama's education speech with the Blogalicious B-Link members at the National Urban League's Centennial Conference.
- Hosting a series of D.C. Women in Social Media panel discussions at Martin Luther King, Jr. Memorial Library.
- Organizing Digital Sisterhood Month, an online and offline celebration that gives women in social media an opportunity to celebrate their connections, conversations, communities, collaborative partnerships, and commerce.
- Naming Shameeka Ayers, The Broke Socialite founder, as Digital Sister of the Year.
- Leveraging my relationships and social capital to conduct a successful crowdfunding campaign on Kickstarter.com that raised money for the publication of my *Digital Sisterhood* book.

❖ 2011

- Using the Digital Sisterhood Network's Facebook and Twitter platforms to promote women's health awareness campaigns that discuss breast cancer, domestic violence, heart health, HIV/AIDS, fitness, mental health, and nutrition.

- Mentoring and training Kamaria Richmond, the Digital Sisterhood Network's Blogger-in-Residence.

- Sharing the YouTube link of Egyptian pro-democracy activist Asmaa Mahfouz's video that helped rally Egyptians to protest in Tahrir Square in Cairo, Egypt with my Facebook friends.

- Learning about the YWCA Canada's Safety Siren, an iPhone app that acts as a rape whistle when the user presses a button or shakes her phone to set off an alarm that automatically dials a friend and sends an email with the user's geo-location on a map.

- Realizing I needed to create a regular schedule of unplugging from my digital life after reading Gwen Bell's *Digital Warriorship* book.

- Laughing while watching Claire Dee Lim's "The Power Object," a comedy webisodes series, and Issa Rae's webisodes series, "The Misadventures of Awkward Black Girl."

- Traveling to Haiti as a Blogger Ambassador for Macy's Heart of Haiti campaign.

- Supporting Manal al-Sharif's Women2Drive Facebook, @women2drive Twitter account, and #women2drive Twitter hashtag campaigns to encourage Saudi Arabian women to protest the ban on women driving their cars in Saudi Arabia.

- Following the tweets of Spelman College President Beverly Daniel Tatum @BDTSpelman.

- Serving as a panelist during the Digital Doyennes: Wisdom from the Women Who Lead in Social Media and Innovation event sponsored by Spelman College's Digital Moving Image Salon and Women in Film & Television Atlanta.

- Answering students' questions at Howard University's New Media Symposium organized by Professor Ada Vilageliu-Diaz.

- Leaving tips about my favorite D.C. places to sip tea and write like Starbucks and Teaism on Foursquare.

- Selecting To the Other Side of Dreaming blog founders Stacey Milbern and Mia Mingus as the 2011 Digital Sisters of the Year.
- Facilitating a Blogger Wellness session at BlogHer's annual conference.
- Meeting Dariela Cruz of Dari Design Studio during the Blogalicious Weekend Conference's networking session and later hiring her to design Digital Sisterhood Month badges.
- Profiling 30 Women in PR and Communications on Digital Sisterhood Network's Facebook and Twitter pages.
- Partnering with Xina Eiland, founder of The Eiland Group, and Julie Ergermayer, owner of Violet Boutique, to sponsor the Digital Sisterhood Network's Fierce Living in Fashion Tweetup.
- Conducting an interview with PR Couture blog founder Crosby Noricks about her book, *Ready to Launch: The PR Couture Guide to Breaking into Fashion PR*, and work in fashion public relations on Digital Sisterhood Radio.

❖ 2012
- Teaching a Fierce Living from Your Creative Heart workshop session at the BlissDom Conference.
- Becoming a passionate Animoto, Instagram, and Pinterest user.
- Being inspired by Spelman College's Women of Color Leadership Conference to establish the Digital Sisterhood Leadership Project that profiles women in social media on Facebook, Pinterest, Twitter, and the Digital Sisterhood Network web.
- Participating as a panelist for the How Social Media Can Shape Your Leadership Brand panel at Spelman College's Eight Annual Women of Color Leadership Conference.
- Discovering Liz Dennery Sanders' SheBrand.com and reading her blog as resource for expanding my personal brand.

- Listening to BlogHer co-founders Elisa Camahort Page and Lisa Stone discuss the power of the BlogHer economy being able to pay 4,250 women and men bloggers $17 million from 2009 to 2011 during the annual BlogHer conference.
- Moderating a Podcasting 101 panel with Deborah Shane and Jasmin Singer at the BlogHer conference.
- Attending the first-ever BlogHer Fashion Show and seeing my digital sister Laurita Tellado get out of her wheelchair and walk the runway as a blogger model.
- Using my blog and social media platforms to express my support for President Barack H. Obama's re-election campaign and First Lady Michelle Obama's initiatives.
- Organizing Yoga for Obama fundraiser classes with my yoga Meetup.com D.C. group and teaching classes in Malcolm X-Meridian Hill Park.
- Joining Women Online's Social Media Sprint Campaign to promote President Obama by live tweeting with other women bloggers and social media influencers during the election debates and final weeks of the 2012 campaign.
- Celebrating my first Fashion Night Out DC with my digital sister Brea Ellis, founder of the What I Wore: Tip to Toe blog, and tweeting our photos from our Adams Morgan and U Street adventures.
- Deciding to launch my lifestyle blog, Ananda@16thandU: A Lifestylista in Love with DC after having so much fun during Fashion Night Out DC and reading Yuli Ziv's *Fashion 2.0* book.
- Sharing my thoughts as a speaker during the Blog Community Jam Session at the Blogalicious Weekend Conference.
- Watching Elayne Fluker's ChicRebellion.tv, the first and only Internet TV network developed by women of color for women of color
- Serving as an advisory board member for and attending DigitalunDivided.com's FOCUS100 Symposium for

thought leaders, entrepreneurs, and innovators who are using emerging technologies to engage Black women.

- Learning about smartphone apps, crowdfunding, interactive games, and webisodes script writing during Women Interactive, a Creative Technology Festival co-sponsored by the Art of Genius Creative Technology Series and Spelman College's Digital Moving Image Salon.
- Partnering with Amy Vernon and other digital women to build the Tech Women Unite! Facebook community.
- Joining AARP's Kitchen Cabinet Blogger Advisory Group for the Caregiving Campaign during National Family Caregivers Month.
- Accepting Willa Shalit's invitation to become an ambassador for her new ethical fashion venture, MaidenNation.com.
- Using the "cash mob" model to develop a "buy local" event with Brea Ellis to support businesses owned by women and people of color in my U Street neighborhood during Digital Sisterhood Month in Washington, D.C.
- Hosting two New York City meet ups during Digital Sisterhood Month.
- Naming the 2012 Digital Sisters of the Year as the "Digital Sisterhood 100."

❖ 2013

- Participating in Tracy Lee Jones' The Feminine Business Model Global Telejam Series to help me solidify my 2013 business and personal development goals.
- Subscribing to Sara Avant Stover's *The Way of the Happy Woman* e-newsletter and reading her book and blog.
- Reading Claudia Chan's blog, email newsletters, and web site that profile the stories of positive and inspiring women.
- Obtaining business and career advice from Melody Biringer's *Flipped It!* And *Craving Success* e-books, Natalie MacNeal's *She Takes on the World* book and web site, Amy Jo Martin's *Renegades Make the Rules*, and Natalie Sission's SuitcaseEntrepreneur.com e-books and resources.

- Serving as a content curator advisor for the Blogalicious Tech Summit.
- Maintaining a regular blogging schedule for my author blog by posting my reflections on Yoga Mondays, Internet Geek Tuesdays, and Creativity Thursdays.
- Profiling women's crowdfunding accomplishments on the Digital Sisterhood Network blog.
- Following the tweets of the "Scandal" ABC television cast and fans with great excitement.
- Attending the Rails Girls DC screening of Ayna Agarwal and Ellora Israaani's "She++" documentary that encourages women and girls to pursue careers in computer science and technology.
- Receiving a scholarship to attend the Rails Girls DC Workshop on coding.
- Being inspired to dream bigger by watching Marie Forleo's Marie TV webisodes.
- Discovering Angela Burt Murray's CocoaFab TV YouTube Channel.
- Watching Tracey Edmonds' AlrightTV YouTube Channel, Ashly Blaine Featherson and Lena Waithe's "Hello Cupid" webisodes series, Danielle Scott-Haughton's "Dear Jesus" webisodes series, and Shakira Scott's "UnFamous" webisodes series.
- Working as a blogger ambassador for AARP's Decide.Create. Share. campaign for women's long-term planning.
- Witnessing the creativity of HaJ's live interactive multimedia performance, "Funnel Cake Flowers and the Urban Chameleons" and using Twitter for audience participation at American University's Katzen Arts Center.
- Being named an author of the 2012-2013 Hot Mommas Project case study library.
- Facilitating two social media leadership sessions and hosting the Multi-Culti community party with Pauline Campos and Dwana De La Cerna at the BlogHer Conference.

Ananda Kiamsha Madelyn Leeke

Digital Sisterhood Notes Section

Digital Sisterhood Notes Section

APPENDIX G

Digital Diva Sheroes and Virtual Mentors

Over the years, I have learned many things from women online. The women who have influenced, inspired, and informed me the most are my Digital Diva Sheroes. I have met some of these women in person and formed relationships that have offered me mentoring support and peer-to-peer learning experiences. Others have become virtual mentors to me.

Below you will find a list of my Digital Diva Sheroes and Virtual Mentors. The list is organized according to my Digital Sisterhood Leadership archetypes. It's long so grab something yummy to sip on as you read it. I encourage you to use the Digital Sisterhood Notes Section to create your own list. Have fun!

1) *Creativistas*
   o Lucrerer Braxton, founder of ArtSlam
   o Kesha Bruce, artist, founder of KeshaBruceStudio.com, gallery director, and writer
   o Ayoka Chenzira, digital media artist, filmmaker, founder of OrdinaryActs.com and Spelman College's Digital Moving Image Salon, and professor
   o Joy Cho, author, designer, and founder of Oh Joy! Blog
   o Dariela Cruz, co-founder of Dari Design Studio and founder of MamiTalks.com
   o Diane Cu, co-founder of WhiteonRice.com and photographer

- o Cathy Delaleu, artist, author, founder of Lyrically I am Yours blog, and poet
- o Claudine Hellmuth, artist, author, and blogger
- o Tara Frey, artist, author, and blogger
- o Sabrina Harvey, co-founder of Friday Girl TV, Art of Genius Technology Series, and Girl Genius Productions
- o Philippa Hughes, founder of PinkLineProject.com
- o Leah Piken Kolidas, artist and founder of CreativeEveryDay.com
- o Thien-Kim Lam, founder of MyCupofCreativetea.com
- o Claire Dee Lim, founder of "The Power Object" webisode series
- o Arielle Loren, founder of Corset Magazine
- o Susan Miller, creator of "The Bestsellers" webisode series
- o Carmen Elena Mitchell, founder of "The Real Girl's Guide to Everything Else" webisode series
- o Kathy Cano-Murillo, founder of CraftyChica.com
- o Stephanie Piche, founder of Mingle Media TV
- o Haj Chenzira-Pinnock, founder of Tickles TV
- o Felicia Pride, author and founder of The Create Daily and Pride Collective
- o Issa Rae, founder of "The Misadventures of Awkward Black Girl"
- o Kelly Rae Roberts, artist, author, and founder of KellyRaeRoberts.com
- o Ashia Sims, co-founder of Friday Girl TV, Art of Genius Technology Series, and Girl Genius Productions
- o Jessica Solomon, founder of The Saartjie Project
- o Sonya Steele, founder of "Celeste Bright" webisode series
- o Daryn Strauss, founder of DigitalChick.tv
- o Mindy Tsonas, artist and founder of WishStudio.com
- o Karen Walrond, author, founder Chookooloonks.com, and photographer
- o Kim Williams, creator of "Unwritten Rules" webisode series
- o Tanekya Word, artist and founder of HybridChic.com

2) *Empiristas*
   o Julie Diaz Asper, co-founder of GigCoin of Social Lens Research
   o Gina Bianchini, co-founder of Ning.com and founder of Mightybell.com
   o Melody Biringer, founder of The Crave Company
   o Kimberly Bryant, founder of BlackGirlsCode.com
   o Jessica Faye Carter, author and founder of OnToour.com
   o Majora Carter, founder of Startup Box: South Bronx
   o Ana Roca Castro, founder of Latinos in Social Media
   o Jacqui Chew, founder of iFusion Marketing
   o Esther Dyson, author, investor, and founder of EDventure
   o Catherine Austin Fitts, founder and President of Solari, Inc.
   o Caterina Flake, co-founder of Flickr
   o Elaine Gittins, founder of Blurb.com
   o Cynthia Good, founder of Little PINK Book
   o Ella Gorgla, founder of I-ELLA
   o Julie Hartz, co-founder of Eventbrite
   o LaShanda Henry, founder of Black Business Women Online and Multiple Shades of You Online
   o Kelly Hoey, co-founder of Women Innovate Mobile
   o Arianna Huffington, founder of The Huffington Post
   o Tara Hunt, author and founder of Buyosphere
   o Deborah Jackson, founder of PlumAlley.co and JumpThru, and co-founder of Women Innovate Mobile
   o Jennifer James, founder of MomBloggersClub.com
   o Jory Des Jardins, co-founder of BlogHer
   o Barbara Jones, co-founder of BlissDom and founder of One2One Network
   o Liza Kindred, founder of ThirdWaveFashion.com
   o Tamara Knetchel, co-founder of Everywhere
   o Danica Kombol, co-founder and managing partner of Everywhere
   o Jessica Lee, co-founder of Polyvore.com
   o Cat Lincoln, co-founder of Clever Girls Collective
   o Natalie MacNeal, founder of SheTakesontheWorld.com

o   Sian Morson, founder of Kollective Mobile
o   Elisa Camahort Page, co-founder of BlogHer
o   Stefani Pomponi, co-founder of Clever Girls Collective
o   Liz Dennery Sanders, founder of SheBrand.com
o   Rashmi Sinha, co-founder of SlideShare.com
o   Natalie Sissions, founder of SuitcaseEntrepreneur.com
o   Martha Stewart, founder of Martha Stewart Living Omnimedia
o   Jai Stone, branding specialist and founder of BlackLoveForum.com and Black Love Mag
o   Lisa Stone, co-founder of BlogHer
o   Deanna Sutton, founder of ClutchMagazine.com
o   Dr. Beverly Daniel Tatum, President of Spelman College
o   Lena West, founder of Influence Expansion
o   Alli Worthington, co-founder of BlissDom

3) *Enchantistas*
o   Brene Brown, author, founder of OrdinaryCourage.com, and research professor
o   Monica Coleman, author, founder of Beautiful Mind blog, minister, and professor
o   Kety Esquivel, principal and co-founder of McCarson Consulting, and digital executive at Fenton
o   Yael Flusberg, author, coach, founder of Y's Elements blog, and yoga teacher
o   Faith Hunter, podcaster and founder of Faith Hunter Yoga and Embrace DC
o   Tracy Lee Jones, founder of The Feminine Business Model
o   Jeannette Kaplun, author and founder of Todobebe.com
o   Alice Langholt, Reiki master practitioner and founder of ReikiAwakening.com
o   Danielle LaPorte, author and founder of White Hot Truth
o   Jennifer Lee, coach and founder of Artizen Coaching
o   Zawadi Nyong'o, founder of ZerobyZawadi.com
o   Lissa Rankin, author, founder of OwningPink.com, and integrative medicine physician
o   Akilah Richards, founder of Execumama.com

- o   Jamie Ridler, coach and founder of Jamie Ridler Studios
- o   Willa Shalit, artist, author, and founder of Fair Winds Trading, Inc. and Maiden Nation
- o   Sara Avant Stover, author of *The Way of the Happy Woman*
- o   Latham Thomas, author, birth coach, founder of Mama Glow and Mama Glow Film Fest, and yoga teacher
- o   Nancy Wait, author of *The Nancy Who Drew* and founder of The Alchemy of Memoir blog
- o   Renita Weems, author, founder of SomethingWithin.com, minister, and professor
- o   Kimberly Wilson, author, founder of Tranquil Space and Tranquility du Jour podcast, and yoga teacher
- o   Oprah Winfrey, founder of Harpo Productions, Inc. and the OWN Network

4) *Empoweristas*
- o   Kelli Anderson, founder of Sojournals Urban Media Network
- o   Valerie Aurora, co-founder of The Ada Initiative
- o   Moya Bailey, founder of Quirky Black Girl social networking site and co-founder of the Crunk Feminists blog
- o   Joanne Bamberger, author, blogger, political writer, and founder of Broad Side Strategies
- o   Amy DuBois Barnett, author and Editor-in-Chief of *Ebony*
- o   Leticia Barr, founder of TechSavvyMama.com
- o   Alex "Skud" Bayley, founder of Geek Feminism blog
- o   Holly Buchanan, author and founder of MarketingtoWomenOnline.com
- o   Kathryn Buford, founder of LiveUnchained.com
- o   Donna Byrd, publisher of TheRoot.com
- o   Monica Calhoun, founder of The Savvy Sista blog
- o   Kat Calvin, co-founder of Blerdology
- o   Boni Candelario, career strategy and empowerment coach and founder of CoachMUp.com
- o   Candice Carpenter, founder of iVillages.com
- o   Claudia Chan, founder of ClaudiaChan.com and S.H.E. Summit

o   Sara Chipps, co-founder of Girl Develop It
o   Cheryl Contee, co-founder of Fission Strategy and founder of JackandJillPolitics.com
o   Corynne Corbett, founder of Beauty Swirl, Chic Jones Media, and ThatBlackGirlSite.com
o   Fanshen Cox, co-founder of Mixed Chicks Podcast
o   Nicole Cutts, founder of Women-Owned Business Wednesdays Facebook group and Vision Quest Retreats, Inc.
o   Jenifer Daniels, founder of TheFriendRaiser.com
o   Jessie Daniels, author, founder of RacismReview.com, and professor
o   April Davis, founder of AroundHarlem.com
o   Tomika DePriest, Executive Director, Office of Communications, Spelman College
o   Heidi Durrow, author and co-founder of Mixed Chicks Podcast
o   Stacey Ferguson, co-founder and chief curator of BeBlogalicious.com
o   Faydra Deon Fields, author, founder of IndAIndex.com, and web consultant
o   Ana Flores, author, co-founder of SpanglishBaby.com, and founder of LatinaBloggersConnect.com
o   Jane Fonda, activist, actress, author, and co-founder of the Women's Media Center
o   Marie Forleo, founder of Marie TV
o   Jill Foster, founder of WomenGrowBusiness.com and Live Your Talk
o   Monique Frausto, founder of Blogs by Latinas and Latina Fashion Bloggers
o   Kathy Korman Frey, founder of HotMommasProject.com and professor
o   Mary Gardiner, co-founder of The Ada Initiative
o   Alexis Pauline Gumbs, author, founder of Broken Beautiful Press blog, professor, and writer
o   Kaliya Hamlin, founder of She's Geeky Unconference

o   Aminah Hanan, executive director of BloggingWhileBrown.
    com and managing editor of MichelleObamaWatch.com
o   Rachel Sterne Haot, chief digital officer of New York City
    and founder of GroundReport.com
o   A. Breeze Harper, author and founder of The Sistah Vegan
    Project blog
o   Kristal High, founder of Politics365
o   Twanna Hines, founder of FunkyBrownChick.com
o   Vanessa Hurst, co-founder of Girl Develop It and founder of
    Developers for Good
o   Nirasha Jaganath, founder of MommyNiriCares.com
o   Lauren Brown Jarvis, founder of DigitalDoyennes.com
o   Niambi Jarvis, founder of HiyaahPower.com and Women for
    Change social networking site
o   Christine Johnson, founder of IamDTech
o   Lynne Johnson, blogger, digital and social media strategist at
    Waggener Edstrom Worldwide, and writer
o   Tara Joyce, founder of The Rise of the Innerpreneur blog
o   Allyson Kapin, founder of WomenWhoTech.com
o   Yalanda Lattimore, founder of DryerBuzz.com
o   Sasha Laundy, founder of Women Who Code
o   Amber Leab, co-founder of Bitch Flicks
o   Sariane Leigh, founder of AnacostiaYogi.com
o   Angelica Perez-Litwin, founder of New Latina
o   Natalie Lue, author and founder of Baggage Reclaim blog
o   Shannon Lynberg, co-founder of Holla Back DC!
o   Kate Hellmuth Martin, co-founder of PRENEUR.net
o   LaShaun Martin, founder of ShootieGirl.net and Mocha
    Moms social media director
o   Issa Mas, author, founder of SingleMamaNYC.com and
    YourSingleParenting.com, and life coach
o   Sarah Massey, founder of Fabulous Women Biz Owners DC
    Group and Massey Media
o   Zerlina Maxwell, Democratic strategist and staff writer for
    Loop21.com

o   Laura Mayes, author, co-founder of Kirtsy.com, and founder of Blog con Queso blog
o   Anissa Mayhew, founder of AimingLow.com and co-founder of InsertEyeRoll.com
o   Erica McGillivary, founder of GeekGirlCon.com
o   Ellen McGirt, Senior Writer at *Fast Company*
o   Cheryl Mayberry McKissack, COO of Johnson Publishing Company, founder of NiaOnline.com, President/CEO of Nia Enterprises, LLC., and author
o   Natalie McNeal, author and founder ofTheFrugalista.com
o   Morra Aarons Mele, founder of Women Online and The Mission List
o   Amy Melrose, founder of Free in DC blog
o   Denene Millner, author, founder of MyBrownBaby.com, and journalist
o   Shireen Mitchell, founder of Digital Sisters, Inc. and Tech Media Swirl
o   Tinu Abayomi-Paul, editor of WomenGrowBusiness.com
o   Melissa Harris-Perry, author, founder of Kitchen Table blog, and professor
o   Pam Perry, author, blogger, and PR coach
o   Jennifer Pozner, author and founder of Women in Media & News
o   Sabrina Ptacin, co-founder of PRENEUR.net
o   Sofia Quintero, author, filmmaker, and founder of Chica Luna Productions
o   Elianne Ramos, host of Latinos in Social Media Twitter party and founder of Speak Hispanic
o   Corvida Raven, founder of SheGeeks.net
o   Adria Richards, founder of ButYouAreAGirl.com
o   Allissa Richardson, founder of MojoMediaWorks.com
o   Deb Rox, author, co-publisher of ShePosts.com, and founder of Platform
o   Liza Sabater, founder of Culture Kitchen Media and The Daily Gotham
o   Reshma Saujani, founder of Girls Who Code

- o Liz Scherer, founder of Flashfree: Not Your Mama's Menopause blog, health journalist, and marketing and social media strategist
- o Marianne Schnall, author and founder of Feminist.com
- o Chai Shenoy, co-founder of Holla Back DC!
- o Aliza Sherman, author, digital strategist, web and social mobile pioneer, and founder of Mediaegg
- o Melissa Silverman, founder of WomenandHollywood.com
- o Veronika Sonsev, founder of Women in Wireless and inSparq.com
- o Roxana Sota, author and co-founder of SpanglishBaby.com
- o Amanda Spann, co-founder of Blerdology
- o Marcia Wade Talbert, Tech Editor and Multimedia Content Producer at *Black Enterprise*
- o Ronnie Tyler, co-founder of BlackandMarriedwithKids.com
- o Ebony Utley, author, founder of TheUtleyExperience.com, and professor
- o Jessica Valenti, author and founder of Feministing.com
- o Lisann Valentin, founder of HerDeepThoughts.com
- o Amy Vernon, digital strategist, founder of Women Tech Unite! Facebook Group, freelance writer, and General Manager for Social Marketing for Internet Media Labs
- o Gloria Ware, founder of Black and Into Green blog
- o Tamar Weinberg, author, digital marketing specialist, and Mashable's Global Advertising Director
- o Taly Weiss, founder of TrendSpotting Trends Agency and marketing trends researcher
- o Kamy Wicoff, author and founder of SheWrites.com
- o Diane Williams, co-founder of Black Author Showcase social networking site
- o Benet Wilson, founder of Aviation Queen blog and journalist
- o Veronica Woods, founder of MySalonScoop.com
- o Jenna Wortham, Tech Reporter at the *New York Times*
- o Ruby Wright, founder of Growing Up Blackxican blog
- o Takeya Young, founder of Core Connection Lifestyle and yoga teacher

o   Nelly Yusupova, founder of TechSpeak for Entrepreneurs and chief technology officer of Webgrrls International

o   Deanna Zandt, author, blogger, and media technologist

5) *Evangelistas*

o   Luvvie Ajai, co-founder of The Red Pump Project

o   Bianca Alexander, co-founder of Conscious.TV

o   Veronica Arreola, founder of Viva La Feminista blog

o   Toni Carey, co-founder of BlackGirlsRun.com

o   Sloane Berrent Davidson, founder of TheCausemopaulitan.com

o   Racquel Dozier, Lupus activist, blogger and founder of LupusinColor.com

o   Tanya Fields, founder of The BLK ProjeK, environmental justice activist, and social entrepreneur

o   Tracey Friley, founder of OneBrownGirl.com and The Passport Party Project

o   Ashley Hicks, co-founder of BlackGirlsRun.com

o   Regina Holliday, artist and founder of Medical Advocacy Blog

o   Bassey Ikpi, author, mental health activist, and founder of The Siwe Project, "No Shame Day," and #NoShame Twitter

o   Ileana Jimenez, educator and founder of FeministTeacher.com

o   Tracy Chiles McGhee, founder of Womanifesting

o   Nicole McLean, breast cancer activist and founder of My Fabulous Boobies blog

o   Stacey Milbern, disabled activist, founder of Leaving Evidence blog, co-founder of To the Other Side of Dreaming blog, and poet

o   Mia Mingus, disabled justice activist and organizer, founder, co-founder of To the Other Side of Dreaming blog, and writer

o   Renee Ross, founder of Cutie Booty Cakes blog, health activist, and runner

o   Yoani Sanchez, activist, author, and founder of Generación Y blog
o   Jasmin Singer, co-founder of OurHenHouse.org and podcaster
o   Katina Stapelton, founder of Butterfly Lessons: Living a Fabulous Life with Lupus, Lupus activist, and political scientist
o   Laurita Tellado, blogger, founder of HoldinOurForAHero.org, and journalist
o   Rae Lewis-Thorton, AIDS activist, author, blogger, and founder of the RLT Collection
o   Suzanne Turner, founder of Feminism 2.0 conference and web site
o   Karyn Watkins, co-founder of The Red Pump Project
o   Tracey Webb, founder of BlacksGiveBack.com
o   Chrysula Winegar, founder of WhenYouWakeUpAMother.com

6) *Flowistas*
o   Gwen Bell, author, global entrepreneur, and yoga teacher
o   Amy Jo Martin, author and founder of ReadySetPause.com
o   Zeenat Merchant-Syal, author, founder of PositiveProvocations.com, and psychologist

7) *Lifestylistas*
o   Abiola Abrams, author, lifestyle journalist, and founder of Abiola.TV
o   Shameeka Ayers, author and founder of The Broke Socialite blog and Lavish: An Unconference for the Lifestyle Social Networker
o   Monica Barnett, founder of Blueprint4Style.com
o   Zandile Blay, founder of AfricaStyleDaily.com
o   Christina Brown, founder of LoveBrownSugar.com
o   Monica Byrd, founder of BabyBlashandBling.com and TheCharmChat.com
o   Lilian Chang, founder of ChineseGrandma.com

o   Harriette Cole, author, founder of Harriette Cole Media and 108Stitches.biz, and lifestyle stylist
o   Kelly Collis, founder of CityShopGirl.com
o   Julia Coney, founder of AllAboutThePretty.net
o   Brea Ellis, founder of What I Wore: Tip to Toe blog
o   Yakini Etheridge, founder of The Prissy Mommy Chronicles blog and RealityTVFashion.com.
o   Jewel Figueras, founder of JewelsFabLife.com
o   Kathryn Finney, author and founder of The Budget Fashionista and DigitalunDivided.com
o   Kiratiana Freelon, author and founder of KiratianaTravels.com
o   Latoicha Givens, founder of LuxeTips.com
o   Krystin Hargrove, founder of BeLoudBeYou.com
o   Maura Hernandez, founder of TheOtherSideofTheTortilla.com
o   Bren Herrera, founder of FlanboyantEats.com
o   Mattie James, founder of Atlanta Style Bloggers, Mattieologie.com, and Style Bloggers of Color
o   Dana Williams-Johnson, founder of Art of Accessories blog
o   Denise Johnson, founder of RainydayDiva.com
o   Marie Denee Leggette, founder of The Curvy Fashionista blog
o   Sondra Lewis, founder of Chic Chocolate blog
o   Danyelle Little, founder of TheCubicleChick.com
o   Katherine Martinez, founder of La Petite Marmoset
o   Jennae Petersen, founder of GreenYourDecor.com
o   Mercedes Sanchez, founder of BeChicMag.com
o   Jacqueline Shaw, author and founder of AfricaFashionGuide.com
o   Trina Small, founder of TheBabyShopaholic.com
o   Nichelle Stephens, founder of Cup Cakes Take the Cake blog
o   Deb Vaughan, founder of Real Girl Runway
o   Patrice Yursik, founder of Afrobella.com

Ananda Kiamsha Madelyn Leeke

Digital Sisterhood Notes Section

Digital Sisterhood Notes Section

List of 2012 Digital Sisters of the Year (Digital Sisterhood 100)

1) *Creativistas*
   - Ayoka Chenzira, digital media artist, filmmaker, founder of OrdinaryDayActs.com and Spelman College's Digital Moving Image Salon, and professor
   - Joy Cho, author, designer, and founder of Oh Joy! blog
   - Dariela Cruz, co-founder of Dari Design Studio and founder of MamiTalks.com
   - Leah Piken Kolidas, artist and founder of Art Every Day Month and CreativeEveryDay.com
   - Claire Dee Lim, founder of "The Power Object" webisode series
   - Arielle Loren, founder of Corset Magazine
   - Kathy Cano-Murillo, author and founder of CraftyChica.com
   - Stephanie Piche, founder of Mingle Media TV
   - Felicia Pride, author and founder of The Create Daily and Pride Collective
   - Issa Rae, founder of "The Misadventures of Awkward Black Girl" webisode series
   - Kelly Rae Roberts, artist, author, and founder of KellyRaeRoberts.com
   - Jessica Solomon, founder of Art In Praxis: Theory+Practice/Art=New Worlds blog and The Saartjie Project
   - Daryn Strauss, founder of Digital Chick TV and "Downsized" webisode series
   - Mindy Tsonas, artist and founder of WishStudio.com

2) *Empiristas*
   - Julie Diaz Asper, co-founder of GigCoin and Social Lens Research
   - Melody Biringer, author and founder of The Crave Company
   - Kimberly Bryant, engineer and founder of BlackGirlsCode.com
   - Majora Carter, founder of Startup Box: South Bronx

- Ana Roca Castro, founder of Latinos in Social Media and Premier Social Media
- Angie Chang, co-founder of Women 2.0
- Shaherose Charania, co-founder of Women 2.0
- Ella Gorgla, founder of I-ELLA
- LaShanda Henry, author and founder of Black Business Women Online and Multiple Shades of You Online
- Kelly Hoey, co-founder of Women Innovate Mobile
- Deborah Jackson, founder of PlumAlley.co and JumpThru, and co-founder of Women Innovate Mobile
- Jory Des Jardins, co-founder of BlogHer
- Danica Kombol, co-founder and managing partner of Everywhere
- Wen Wen Lam, co-founder of Women 2.0
- Sian Morson, founder of Kollective Mobile
- Elisa Camahort Page, co-founder of BlogHer
- Veronika Sonsev, co-founder of Women Innovate Mobile and founder of inSparq.com and Women in Wireless
- Shivani Sopory, co-founder of Women 2.0
- Lisa Stone, co-founder of BlogHer
- Dr. Beverly Daniel Tatum, author and President of Spelman College

3) *Empoweristas*
- Joanne Bamberger, author and founder of PunditMom.com
- Sara Chipps, co-founder of Girl Develop It
- Stacey Ferguson, co-founder and chief curator of BeBlogalicious.com and founder of Justice Fergie Lifestyle Media
- Ana Flores, author, co-founder of SpanglishBaby.com, and founder of LatinaBloggersConnect.com
- Kathy Korman Frey, founder of HotMommasProject.com and professor
- Alexis Pauline Gumbs, author, founder of Broken Beautiful Press blog, professor, and writer
- Kristal High, founder of Politic365

- Vanessa Hurst, co-founder of Girl Develop It and founder of Developers for Good
- Lauren Brown Jarvis, founder of DigitalDoyennes.com, National Communications Director for the New Leaders Council, and writer for Examiner.com and The Huffington Post
- Christine Johnson, founder of IamDTech
- Tara Joyce, author and founder of The Rise of the Innerpreneur blog
- Allyson Kapin, founder of WomenWhoTech.com
- Christine Koh, founder of BostonMamas.com and PoshPeacock.com
- Yalanda Lattimore, founder of DryerBuzz.com
- Sarah Massey, founder of Fabulous Women Biz Owners DC and Massey Media
- Anissa Mayhew, founder of AimingLow.com and co-founder of InsertEyeRoll.com
- Morra Aarons Mele, founder of Women Online
- Shireen Mitchell, founder of Digital Sisters, Inc. and Tech Media Swirl
- Tinu Abayomi-Paul, editor of WomenGrowBusiness.com
- Elianne Ramos, host of Latinos in Social Media Twitter party and founder of Speak Hispanic
- Allissa Richardson, founder of MojoMediaWorks.com, journalist, and professor
- Liz Scherer, founder of Flashfree: Not Your Mama's Menopause blog, health journalist, and marketing and social media strategist
- Aliza Sherman, author, digital strategist, web and social mobile pioneer, and founder of Mediaegg
- Marcia Wade Talbert, Tech Editor and Multimedia Content Producer at *Black Enterprise*
- Ericka Tinsley, founder of The Swarthy Suite, Fro-Fi Collective, and Chocolate Chat Atlanta
- Ronnie Tyler, co-founder of BlackandMarriedwithKids.com and Tyler New Media

- Ebony Utley, author, founder of TheUtleyExperience.com, Ms. Magazine blogger, and professor
- Amy Vernon, digital strategist, founder of Women Tech Unite! Facebook Group, freelance writer, and General Manager for Social Marketing for Internet Media Labs
- Gloria Ware, founder of Black and Into Green blog
- Veronica Woods, founder of BookYourChairSolid.com and MySalonScoop.com

4) *Enchantistas*
  - Monica Coleman, author, founder of Beautiful Mind blog, minister, and professor
  - Kety Esquivel, digital executive at Fenton Communications and TEDxAdamsMorganWomen convener
  - Faith Hunter, founder of Faith Hunter Yoga and Embrace Yoga, podcaster, and writer
  - Jeannette Kaplun, author and founder of Hispana Global and Todobebe.com
  - Jennifer Lee, author, coach, and founder of Artizen Coaching and Life Unfolds blog
  - Zawadi Nyong'o, founder of ZerobyZawadi.com
  - Akilah Richards, author and founder of Execumama.com, The Lightcaster's Project and The Life Design Agency
  - Jamie Ridler, coach and founder of Jamie Ridler Studios
  - Willa Shalit, artist, author, founder of Fairwinds Trading, Inc., and co-founder of MaidenNation.com
  - Kimberly Wilson, author, eco-designer, founder of Tranquil Space and Tranquility du Jour blog and podcast, and yoga teacher

5) *Evangelistas*
  - Luvvie Ajayi, co-founder of The Red Pump Project, founder of Awesomely Luvvie blog, and social media strategist and trainer
  - Veronica Arreola, founder of Viva La Feminista blog

- Sloane Berrent Davidson, founder of TheCausemopolitan. com
- Tracey Friley, founder of OneBrownGirl.com and The Passport Party Project
- Regina Holliday, artist and founder of Medical Advocacy blog
- Ileana Jimenez, educator and founder of FeministTeacher. com
- Nicole McLean, breast cancer activist and founder of My Fabulous Boobies blog
- Laurita Tellado, blogger, founder of HoldinOurForAHero. org, and journalist
- Suzanne Turner, founder of Feminism 2.0 and Turner Strategies
- Karyn Watkins, co-founder of The Red Pump Project and founder of TheFabulousGiver.com
- Chrysula Winegar, communications consultant and founder of WhenYouWakeUpAMother.com

6) *Flowistas*
- Gwen Bell, author, global entrepreneur, and yoga teacher
- Zeenat Merchant-Syal, author, founder of PositiveProvocations.com, and psychologist

7) *Lifestylistas*
- Monica Byrd, founder of BabyBlashandBling.com and TheCharmChat.com
- Lilian Chang, founder of ChineseGrandma.com
- Julia Coney, founder of AllAboutThePretty.net and yoga teacher
- Jewel Figueras, founder of JewelsFabLife.com
- Kiratiana Freelon, author and founder of KiratianaTravels. com
- Latoicha Givens, founder of LuxeTips.com
- Maura Hernandez, founder of TheOtherSideofTheTortilla. com

- Mattie James, founder of Atlanta Style Bloggers, Mattieologie.com, and Style Bloggers of Color
- Marie Denee Leggette, author and founder of The Curvy Fashionista blog
- Katherine Martinez, founder of La Petite Marmoset
- Mercedes Sanchez, founder of BeChicMag.com
- Jacqueline Shaw, author and founder of AfricaFashionGuide. com
- Deb Vaughan, founder of Real Girl Runway blog

© Leigh Mosley

AUTHOR INTERVIEW

Q: In your writing, you tell stories. How did you become a storyteller?

AKML: I grew up around women who loved to tell stories about their lives. My grandmother, great aunt, and mother shared photo albums, scrapbooks, clothing, jewelry, and memorabilia from events they attended to illustrate their stories. Their stories were told so often I memorized them. Eventually, they were embedded into the tapestry of my life. In high school, college, and law school, I proudly wore their vintage clothing and jewelry with my outfits and told stories about the items to my friends. I still wear these items and share stories. Wearing their things reminds me of who I am and where I come from. It connects me to them at all times.

Q: This book is your second memoir. Who are your favorite memoirists?

AKML: Dr. Maya Angelou is the first memoirist I read in junior high school. I love how Dr. Angelou tells her life stories in a series of books. I adore how Alice Walker and Ntozake Shange have used poetry to tell their personal stories. My friend and activist/artist/scholar Tim'm West's poetical memoir gave me freedom to write my first memoir. I also enjoy reading memoirs written by feminist scholar and cultural critic bell hooks, artist Faith Ringgold, and yoga teacher Cyndi Lee.

Q: What prompted you to write this book?

AKML: In 2009, a publisher (that was on my dream list of publishers) contacted me to explore the possibility of entering into a book contract about how the Internet has impacted women's creativity. Thrilled and excited, I entered into a round of discussions with the publisher. She introduced me to two writing mentors who helped me flush out my ideas for a book outline. I shared the *Sisterhood the Blog* book outline with her and launched a blog, Facebook group, and Twitter account to begin writing the book. A few weeks later, the publisher lost interest. I tried several times to follow up, but did not receive a response. Devastated is the best word to describe how I felt.

My writing mentors encouraged me to write and self-publish the book. So I dived deep into my new blog and distributed its content on my social media sites. A few months later, I added a podcast to the mix. Through my blog, podcast, and social media sites, I was able to interview and profile a diverse group of women in social media and technology. When I attended local and national conferences, events, and meet ups, I used my video camera and audio podcast app to record my interviews. These efforts expanded my understanding of the roles women play in the digital space.

My focus for the book changed after I attended the BlogHer annual conference's closing keynote, "How to Use Your Voice, Your Platform and Your Power," featuring PBS anchor Alison Stewart, White House Project founder Marie Wilson, author and activist Gloria Feldt, and journalist and environmentalist P. Simran Sethi, in 2010. Listening to these women's stories convinced me to write a memoir about my online journey and how women have influenced, informed, and inspired my digital experiences.

That same year, I changed the title of the book, blog, podcast, and social media to Digital Sisterhood after I conducted a series of interviews with women bloggers about their relationships with women in social media at the Blogalicious Weekend Conference.

Q: Who did you write this book for?

AKML: I wrote the book for women between the ages of 18 to 76 who spend time in the digital space blogging, building community, chatting, coding, creating webisodes and videos, crowdfunding, developing mobile apps, engaging in commerce, giving back by supporting social good campaigns, hosting online events, liking on Facebook, mentoring, pinning on Pinterest, podcasting, posting photos on Flickr and Instagram, reading blogs, publishing books, running businesses, serving as social media leaders, sharing information, teaching, tweeting 140 characters or less on Twitter, watching videos, and visiting web sites. I also wrote the book for women and girls who need greater access to technology and training.

Q: What do you want readers to gain from this book?

AKML: I want my readers to take what they find useful in the book and use it in a positive way. I hope my women readers are inspired to explore, celebrate, share, and publish their own stories about being online and the Digital Sisterhood connections they have made with other women. I hope they will publish their stories on blogs and in books. I want more women to write and publish books about their online lives, businesses, social good campaigns, and thought leadership.

Q: Did you use any research data to identify your niche audience?

AKML: I used BlogHer's *Social Media Matters Study* which reported that 87 million women between the ages of 18 to 76 were online in 2011. The BlogHer study also reported that 69 million women used social media weekly, 80 million women used social media monthly, and 55 million women read blogs monthly. When I read this data, I realized these women have created a powerful digital footprint as communicators, connectors, community builders, tech creators, early adopters, and influencers.

Q: Tell us about your journey in embracing the Internet. How did your digital footprint begin?

AKML: My digital footprint began when I logged onto the LexisNexis research service as a first-year law student at Howard University School of Law in August 1986. It marked the beginning of my Internet geek path. My Internet experiences have been greatly influenced by the social connections women have made online and offline. Through them, I have witnessed the growth and expansion of women's presence and power on the World Wide Web. Women are making digital herstory with blogs, books, businesses, careers, coding and software development projects, conferences, events, Facebook, Flickr, Foursquare, Google+, Instagram, LinkedIn, live streaming, meet up groups, mobile apps, online communities, online magazines, organizations, Pinterest, podcasts, Twitter, videos, webinars, web sites, and webisodes.

Q: What are your favorite social media tools?

AKML: That's a hard one. I love so many. Right now, my favorites are all visual: Animoto, Flickr, Google+ Hangout, Instagram, Pinterest, and YouTube.

Q: In your first memoir, That Which Awakens Me, you discussed how you managed your bouts of writer's block. Did you encounter writer's block while writing this book?

AKML: Yes. I struggled to write this book. My ego wanted the writing journey to be different from my previous experiences. I thought it should be smooth, easy, and orderly. I tried really hard to convince myself I could avoid the many days and weeks where sentences died as soon as they were written. Eventually, I realized I needed an intervention. I turned to the words of my writing mentor,

Marita Golden. In her book, *The Word: Black Writers Talk About the Transformative Power of Reading and Writing*, Golden writes, "Very often in the writing of a book, you're struggling with it for a long time, and then there's a moment that you know that you've broken the back of the material, and that all the writing from that point will be clear and dead on." That moment came to me many times through the act of surrender.

When I stopped trying to make the words conform to what my brain wanted and allowed my heart to open and my spirit to go with the flow of the creative process, I began to accept and understand a series of six lessons:

- Lesson #1—Don't pretend you can write this book without experiencing writer's block.
- Lesson #2—This writing journey is filled with struggles. Some big. Some medium. Some small. Accept them.
- Lesson #3—Surrender and stop running from the discomfort of having writer's block. Just be with it.
- Lesson #4—Unplug, get still, and practice mindfulness meditation. Include yoga and Reiki healing touch.
- Lesson #5—In the stillness, allow your spirit, heart, mind, and body to relax and become open to hearing your intuition. Ask what you need to know, say, and do to overcome your writer's block.
- Lesson #6—Trust your gut. Stay alert for the answers. They will come. Keep a piece of paper and a pen handy. You'll be writing soon!

Q: In addition to the lessons learned through the act of surrendering, did you have any other aha moments that helped you overcome your writer's block?

AKML: Even though *Digital Sisterhood* is my third book and I have a regular writing practice, I still have moments where I trip and fall into the potholes of my own fears. During one of my falls, I found

337

comfort in the remarks made by Valerie Jarrett, White House Senior Advisor and Chair of the White House Council on Women and Girls at Facebook Live's Women in Technology Panel held on April 20, 2011. Jarrett stated, "If you are following your passion, if you are doing what excites you, you're doing a great job, recognize yourself." Her words inspired me to incorporate mandatory moments of celebration into my creative process that allowed me to recognize and honor each time I finished a chapter.

Q: What were some of the creative inspirations that helped you write this book?

AKML: When I came across Sunni Brown, the founder of BrightSpot I.D., who was featured as one of the *100 Most Creative People in Business* in the June 2011 issue of *Fast Company*, I knew I had discovered a source of creative inspiration. Brown uses doodling to help her clients expand their brainstorming and collaborative efforts. Her comments were empowering: "Visual language is one of your best friends. Giving an idea shape and a visual representation makes it come to fruition." They led me to use *The Right-Brain Business Plan: A Creative, Visual Map for Success* by Jennifer Lee, a blogger friend and the founder of Artizen Coaching.

Lee's *The Right-Brain Business Plan* gave me "permission to create wildly" and to use a "visual approach to clarifying the big picture" for this book. Using my right-brain gifts of imagination and intuition helped me chip away at my writer's block. I returned to a familiar and fun practice: making a vision board. Creating a "Big Vision Collage" in a sketch book from CVS based on Lee's guidance helped me use visual language to develop affirmations and an action plan for my book. My "Big Vision Collage" sketch book became my launching pad for knowing and believing I could complete and publish my memoir authentically and fearlessly.

Q: What are some of your favorite creativity books?

AKML: My favorites include:

- *Coming Out The Wilderness: A Memoir of A Black Woman Artist* by Estella Conwill Majozo,
- *Making Your Creative Mark* by Eric Maisel,
- *Taking Flight: Inspiration and Techniques to Give Your Creative Spirit Wings* by Kelly Rae Roberts,
- *The Artist's Way: A Spiritual Path to Higher Creativity* by Julia Cameron,
- *The 12 Secrets of Highly Creative Women: A Portable Mentor* by Gail McMeekin, and
- *We Flew over the Bridge: The Memoirs of Faith Ringgold* by Faith Ringgold.

Q: What's next for you?

AKML: I have a six-word memoir that describes what's next: *Fierce Living. Too Bold for Boundaries.* It starts with REST, followed by healthy eating and living, spending time with positive and nurturing people, and expressing and sharing my gifts and talents with others.

© Leigh Mosley

AUTHOR BIO

The best way to describe Ananda Kiamsha Madelyn Leeke is with a six-word memoir. Yoga + Creativity + Internet Geek = Ananda Leeke. Leeke is a lawyer turned "Jill of many trades:" innerpreneur, author, artist, coach, and yoga teacher. Her mission is "Empowering U2BU through creativity coaching, Reiki, self-care, social media, volunteerism, and yoga." Since 2005, she has used her blogs to express her mission, advocate for social good, build community, share information, promote her books and events, and market her services. Currently, she serves as a blogger ambassador for AARP, Everywhere Society, Macy's Heart of Haiti Campaign, and Maiden Nation.

In 2010, her passion for women's issues, building community, and the Internet inspired her to create the Digital Sisterhood Network, a media channel that celebrates women in social media and technology through leadership, lifestyle, and living well initiatives. She is a frequent speaker at conferences sponsored by Blogalicious, BlogHer, Howard University, Ignite DC, and Spelman College. *Black Enterprise* named her as one of the Black Women in Tech You Should Follow on Twitter in 2011. The Hot Mommas Project, a women's leadership research venture housed at the George Washington University School of Business, selected her as an author for its 2012-2013 case study library.

For more than 20 years, Leeke has been actively pursuing her career as an author and artist. Through her poetry chap books and participation in the Washington, D.C. arts movement, her poetry appeared in *Beyond the Frontier: African American Poetry for the 21st Century* (2002). She penned *Love's Troubadours—Karma: Book One*, a novel (2007) and *That Which Awakens Me: A Creative Woman's Poetic Memoir of Self-Discovery* (2009). Her six-word memoir was published in *It All Changed in an Instant: More Six-Word Memoirs by Writers Famous & Obscure* (2010).

Her mixed media collages, wire sculptures, and paintings have been exhibited in the Washington D.C. metropolitan area, New York City, North Carolina, and Kentucky. Her artwork was featured in *Heart and Soul* in 2001 and often reflects her passion for issues affecting people of color and women. In 2002, she created and donated "Our Womanist Spirit" and "I am my sista's keeper wire" sculpture collections to The Women's Collective, an HIV/AIDS direct services organization. She has worked as an artist-in-residence for Smith Center for Healing and the Arts at Howard University Hospital (2003-2009), and is currently serving wounded warriors at the Walter Reed National Military Medical Center.

Morgan State University, Howard University School of Law, and Georgetown University Law Center are her alma maters. While at Morgan, she joined Sigma Gamma Rho Sorority, Inc. She is also a member of All Souls Unitarian Church, Insight Meditation Community of Washington's People of Color Sangha, National League of American Pen Women, and Yoga Alliance. She lives in Washington, D.C. To learn more about her, visit www.anandaleeke.com.

Connect with Ananda
- Web Site: anandaleeke.com
- Email: kiamshaleeke@yahoo.com
- Amazon: amazon.com/author/anandaleeke
- Author Blog: authoranandaleeke.wordpress.com
- Digital Sisterhood Network Blog: digitalsisterhood.wordpress.com
- Lifestylista Blog: anandaleeke.tumblr.com
- Facebook: facebook.com/pages/Ananda-Leeke/68996700906 and facebook.com/digitalsisterhood
- Flickr: flickr.com/photos/anandaleeke
- Instagram: instagram.com/anandaleeke
- LinkedIn: linkedin.com/in/anandaleeke

- Pinterest: pinterest.com/anandaleeke
- Twitter: @anandaleeke and @digitalsisterhd
- Twitter Book Hashtag: #DigitalSisterhood
- Twitter Weekly Hashtags: #YogaMonday, #InternetGeek Tuesday, #DigitalSisterhood Wednesday, and #CreativityThursday
- YouTube: youtube.com/user/anandaleeke

Hire Ananda

- Brand Ambassador/Spokesperson for campaigns that promote the arts, caregiving, creativity, cultural diversity, entrepreneurship, fashion, health and wellness, leadership, meditation, personal development, social good, social media, technology, women's issues, world culture and travel, and yoga.

- Creativity Coach for creative professionals, entrepreneurs, innerpreneurs, nonprofit and social justice leaders, and organizations

- Freelance Writer and Speaker on topics such as blogging, caregiving, creativity, crowdfunding, cultural diversity, entrepreneurship, expressive arts, health and wellness, leadership, meditation, personal development, reinvention, self-publishing, social good campaigns, social media, technology, women's issues, world culture and travel, and yoga

- Instructor or Workshop Facilitator on topics including blogging, creativity, crowdfunding, expressive arts, health and wellness, leadership, personal development, self-publishing, social media, spirituality, women's issues, and yoga